AFRICAN WORLD HISTORIES

Cosmopolitan Africa, c.1700–1875

AFRICAN WORLD HISTORIES

Series Editor
Trevor R. Getz, San Francisco State University

African World Histories is a series of retellings of some of the most commonly discussed episodes of the African and global past from the perspectives of Africans who lived through them. Accessible yet scholarly, African World Histories gives students insights into African experiences concerning many of the events and trends that are commonly discussed in the history classroom.

Titles in the Series

Published
Cosmopolitan Africa, 1700–1875
Trevor R. Getz, San Francisco State University

Colonial Africa, 1884–1994
Dennis Laumann, University of Memphis

Forthcoming
Slavery and the Atlantic Slave Trade, 1400–1800
Kwasi Konadu, City University of New York
Trevor Getz, San Francisco State University

Sovereignty and Struggle, 1945–1994
Jonathan T. Reynolds, Northern Kentucky University
Christopher Saunders, University of Cape Town

Africanizing Democracies, 1980–Present
Alicia Decker, Purdue University
Andrea Arrington, University of Arkansas

AFRICAN WORLD HISTORIES

Cosmopolitan
Africa
c.1700–1875

Trevor R. Getz

San Francisco State University

New York   Oxford
OXFORD UNIVERSITY PRESS

Oxford University Press is a department of the University of Oxford. It furthers the
University's objective of excellence in research, scholarship, and education by
publishing worldwide.

Oxford   New York
Auckland   Cape Town   Dar es Salaam   Hong Kong   Karachi
Kuala Lumpur   Madrid   Melbourne   Mexico City   Nairobi
New Delhi   Shanghai   Taipei   Toronto

With offices in
Argentina   Austria   Brazil   Chile   Czech Republic   France   Greece
Guatemala   Hungary   Italy   Japan   Poland   Portugal   Singapore
South Korea   Switzerland   Thailand   Turkey   Ukraine   Vietnam

For titles covered by Section 112 of the US Higher Education Opportunity
Act, please visit www.oup.com/us/he for the latest information about
pricing and alternate formats.

Published by Oxford University Press
198 Madison Avenue, New York, NY 10016
www.oup.com

Oxford is a registered trademark of Oxford University Press.

Library of Congress Cataloging-in-Publication Data

Getz, Trevor R.
African world histories : cosmopolitan Africa, c.1700–1875 / Trevor R. Getz.
    p. cm.
Includes index.
ISBN 978-0-19-976470-9
1. Africa—History—To 1884. 2. Africa—Social conditions—18th century. 3. Africa—Social
conditions—19th century. I. Title.
DT27.G48 2012
960.22—dc23
2012017009

About the Cover: This is a detail from the Keiskamma Tapestry, created by weavers in the Eastern Cape Province of South Africa to Commemorate the "Cattle Killing" episode of 1855–1856.
This particular panel depicts the aftermath of the slaughter of living cattle and the hope for return
of ancestral cattle. The tapestry is in the custody of the South African Parliament, and is owned
by Standard Bank of South Africa.

9 8 7 6 5 4 3 2 1
Printed in the United States of America
on acid-free paper

CONTENTS

Maps and Figures

Maps

Figures

About the Author

Trevor R. Getz is Professor of History at San Francisco State University. He is the author of *Abina and the Important Men* (2011) and *Slavery and Reform in West Africa* (2004), as well as coauthor of textbooks in world and African history.

Series Introduction

The African World Histories series presents a new approach to teaching and learning for African history and African studies courses. Its main innovation is to interpret African and global experiences from the perspectives of the Africans who lived through them. By integrating accounts and representations produced or informed by Africans with accessible scholarly analysis at both local and global levels, African World Histories gives students insight into Africans' understandings and experiences of such episodes as the Atlantic slave trade, the growth of intercontinental commerce and the industrial revolution, colonialism, and the Cold War. The authors in this series look at these episodes through the lenses of culture, politics, social organization, daily life, and economics in an integrated format informed by recent scholarly studies as well as primary source materials. Unlike those of many textbooks and series, the authors of African World Histories actively take positions on major questions, such as the centrality of violence in the colonial experience, the cosmopolitan nature of precolonial African societies, and the importance of democratization in Africa today. Underlying this approach is the belief that students can succeed when presented with relatively brief, jargon-free interpretations of African societies that integrate Africans' perspectives with critical interpretations and that balance intellectual rigor with broad accessibility.

This series is designed for use in both the world history and the African history/studies classroom. As an African history/studies teaching tool it combines continentwide narratives with emphases on specific, localized, and thematic stories that help demonstrate wider trends. As auxiliary texts for the world history classroom, the volumes in this series can help to illuminate important episodes in the global past from the perspectives of Africans, adding complexity and depth, as well as facilitating intellectual growth for students. Thus they will help world history students not only understand that the human past was "transnational" and shared, but also see how it was understood differently by different groups and individuals.

African World Histories is the product of a grand collaboration. The authors include scholars from around the world and across Africa. Each volume is reviewed by multiple professionals in African history and related fields. The excellent team of editors at Oxford University Press, led by Charles Cavaliere, put a great deal of effort into commissioning, reviewing, and bringing these volumes to publication. Finally, we all stand on the shoulders of early giants in the field, including Cheikh Anta Diop, Joseph Ki-Zerbo, Jan Vansina, and Roland Oliver.

— TREVOR R. GETZ, SERIES EDITOR

Introduction

In *The Rise of the West*, the classic history of the world written by the celebrated world historian William H. McNeill between 1936 and 1962, the eighteenth and early nineteenth centuries are described as the period when the fulcrum of world history shifted from Asia to Europe. "By 1700," McNeill wrote, "the wealth and power at Europe's command clearly surpassed anything that other civilized communities on earth could muster." The story of the world in the 150 years that followed was one in which Europe led the way in innovations—the birth of liberalism, the growth of science, the industrial revolution. By contrast, Africa was depicted as a backward and stagnant region that "by [1850]...[c]onstituted by far the largest single barbarian reservoir left in the world."

It is a sign of the great progress in the study of history that McNeill, decades later, would look back with regret upon this depiction of Africa. In 1990, he wrote that he generally felt the underlying arguments in his book were sound, but "an exception is Africa, where the scholarship of the past twenty-five years has revealed a far more complex interplay of people and cultures than was accessible when I wrote *The Rise of the West*."

McNeill's reversal reflects the wider appreciation among historians of the last few decades that Africa was not the dark continent populated by savages depicted in popular books, movies, and travelogues. The world history textbooks that have been written since *Rise of the West*, for example, have progressively come to include more and more about the economies, political organization, and social experiences of both northern and sub-Saharan African societies. Two episodes that they never leave out are the Atlantic slave trade and formal European colonialism. These two stories sometimes seem to define the modern African experience and to follow one after the other quite seamlessly. The Atlantic slave trade (the focus of volume 1 of this series) peaked in the eighteenth century and then declined following the British abolition of 1807–1808, but it only really ended in the 1880s as the trade to Cuba and Brazil was cut off. Formal colonialism (the focus of volume

3 of this series) can be said to have antecedents in the seventeenth-century expansion of Dutch-speaking settlers in southern Africa and the French conquest of Algeria in the 1830s, but the systematic conquest and domination of African territory only began in the 1880s, just as the last Atlantic slave-trading voyages ended. Together, these two trends tell a story of suffering and violence that–as the Afro-Guyanese scholar Walter Rodney and many others since have argued–seems to resonate in the political, economic, and sociocultural problems faced by African societies today.

However these are not the *only* stories to be told of the modern African past, and in this book I suggest an alternate interpretation of the 175 years leading up to the formal colonization of Africa by Europeans. My argument, without ignoring the impact of the Atlantic slave trade that is the focus of volume 1 of this series, is that Africans between 1700 and 1850 pursued lives, constructed social settings, forged trading links, and imagined worlds that were sophisticated, flexible, and well adapted to the increasingly global and fast-paced interactions of this period. It is this particular story that I call "cosmopolitan Africa."

The term "cosmopolitan" is usually applied to individuals within a society who are well traveled, worldly, accepting of difference, adaptable to new ideas, and appreciative of new experiences. However, these phrases can also be used to describe certain communities and societies in particular places and times. Cosmopolitan societies tend to include members from diverse backgrounds, including some born outside the community. They tend to be both flexible enough to change or respond to new ideas and people and open to internal differences of experience and worldview. They usually have strategies for integrating new ideas and populations and accommodating them without requiring complete assimilation.

By "cosmopolitan," I mean to indicate two key African realities in this period. First, Africans were connected to each other and to other parts of the world by trade, the exchange of ideas, and the migration of peoples. These connections included not only the vast Atlantic trading network often portrayed in histories of this era but also connections across the Mediterranean and Red Seas and the Indian Ocean and equally importantly spanning large regions of the African continent. Second, African societies were flexible and complex enough to deal with the influx of new ideas and movement of peoples that these networks necessitated. The old idea of Africans as stagnant and bound by unchanging traditions simply does not accurately portray the many and rapidly changing styles of social and political organization that Africans constructed in this period.

However, it must be said up front that there are limits to this characterization of precolonial African societies as cosmopolitan. First, although I have chosen in this book to stress the worldly and flexible nature of African societies in this period, in every case local conditions mattered, and to varying degrees there was at times resistance to change and outside ideas within these societies. These conservative impulses, while less pronounced than in the colonial system that would follow the 1880s, were present in these societies just as they are always present in human communities. In fact, skilled readers may identify the fact that, while pursuing accuracy, I am also pushing the argument somewhat to its limits for this period. This is partly an attempt to undo the damage of preconceptions and scholarly arguments that precolonial African societies were merely "traditional" and "tribal" by pointing out the ways in which they organized flexible and complex webs of identity and organization.

The idea that Africans all lived and had always lived in rudimentary, hereditary tribes was the product of the colonial period. In order to justify their rule, and also to make ruling Africans easier, twentieth-century colonizers developed the narratives of Africans as "tribal" peoples, living without civilized or democratic forms of government. Europeans (and by extension North Americans) thus learned through official publications and popular culture that Africans were ruled by despotic "chiefs". They were primitives whose "villages" did not produce much of value. Indeed, they had few goods until Europeans arrived with their manufactured products, which were eagerly snapped up.

This once-dominant picture of the African past is, of course, inaccurate. As we will see later, eighteenth-century Africa was a diverse continent possessing populations that lived in many types of social structures, few of which could be accurately described as tribal. Their societies were governed by interlocking systems of power and authority, and chiefs, where they existed, were rarely powerful enough to be despotic. Africans of this period lived in cities, towns, extended settlement patterns, and only sometimes villages. They produced numerous goods for their own needs, as well as many that were deeply desired outside of the continent. Indeed, the story we often tell of African tribes, chiefs, and villages tells us more about how Europeans thought of themselves in the period of colonization than of the realities in Africa prior to their coming. By promoting these ideas about

Africans, Europeans of this period were really expressing their right to rule because they had "nations," "parliaments," and "cities" and thus imagined the people whom they ruled must have had none of these things.

The argument in this book—that African societies were diverse, flexible, and cosmopolitan—is built on evidence of the African past that directly contradicts these arguments. That this evidence was brought to light over the past half century or so is the direct result of several changes in the profession of history that began in the 1960s. First, the European colonial rule of Africa that had supported the narrative of an unhistorical and primitive Africa has ended. In its wake, African scholars and others studying the continent have proved without a doubt the complexity and richness of Africa's past. Second, these historians and others have in the subsequent decades undertaken a shift in the profession from a political focus on "big events" to two other approaches to studying the past. We can call the first of these "social history." Social historians seek to describe how humans *organized* their societies and how they *experienced* them. The second we call "cultural history." Cultural historians emphasize the way humans in particular places and times have *understood* and discussed their life experiences and social settings through written documents, oral expression, and the making of images and arts.

This volume utilizes these techniques and builds on the work of three generations of scholars of and from Africa who have challenged the idea of Africa as barbaric and unchanging. Yet it also points out some problems with the work of many of these scholars. In fighting against the argument that Africans had no nations, parliaments, or cities, some contemporary historians have made the error of endorsing the categories of value chosen by the colonizers. Even while arguing that Africans had a higher place in them, they nevertheless still implicitly accepted those attributes of "civilization" used by Europeans to rank the world.

I seek to step away from this trap by making use of new research based on careful reading of Africans' oral histories and traditions, written documents, and images of or from the eighteenth century. I am not seeking to argue that Africans were exceptional or distinct, that they shared a particular and unique experience, or to compare them to people in other places and times. Rather, I am trying to report and interpret Africans' experiences, the worlds they constructed, and the worldviews through which they saw them in both their diversity and their uniformity. This analysis is based on the sources from this period and my reading of the work of formally trained historians, as well as the inheritors of these traditions and texts. Scholars like Ifa Amadiume, Jan Vansina, Neil Kodesh, John Thornton, and Jeff Pieres have acted as interpreters as well as researchers, seeking to balance our desire to understand the worlds Africans constructed with the need to present those histories in Africans' own terms. However, they could not have done so without the help of Africans who also served as preservers and interpreters of the past. We owe a debt to both of these groups.

ACKNOWLEDGMENTS

I would like to thank the following people who reviewed the manuscript at various stages of its development:

Wayne Ackerson, Salisbury University

Esperanza Brizuela-Garcia, Montclair State University

Laura J. Mitchell, University of California, Irvine

Maxim Matusevich, Seton Hall University

G. Ugo Nwokeji, University of California, Berkeley

Ordering Their Worlds

A PLACE TO BEGIN

Where does one begin a volume that seeks to help readers reenvision African societies in the period 1750–1875? There are several answers to this question, depending on how one sees the world as operating. It might be appropriate to begin with local economies and links to global trade, or political structures, or perhaps intellectual and cultural pursuits. These are important topics, and they form the core themes of subsequent chapters. This chapter touches on all of them, but it is more about something we can call "society," which means it is about how Africans of this period chose to construct the institutions and relationships that shaped their daily lives. This is the first topic in this book for several reasons.

First, an exploration of society exposes readers to a series of eighteenth-century African societies that were organized and understood by their inhabitants in ways very different than our own, but nevertheless were adapted to their citizens' needs to interact with both their local environments and neighboring or faraway societies. This evidence will hopefully encourage readers to abandon those outmoded and inaccurate models of Africa as a place of chiefs, villages, and tribes.

Second, by focusing on the ways African societies were organized in the early eighteenth century, this chapter lays the groundwork for an understanding of how and why Africans chose to act in the big events and trends covered by later chapters in this volume: the rise of Western-style capitalism and its ideologies, changes in Islamic and Christian practices and faith, the industrial revolution, and the challenge of intellectual modernity. It is for this reason that this chapter generally focuses on the early eighteenth century (1700–1750), and even reaches back somewhat into the previous century, whereas the subsequent chapters generally begin around 1750. In fact, as this chapter establishes, eighteenth- and nineteenth-century African cosmopolitan societies were the culmination of centuries of interaction and adaptation.

Finally, this chapter helps to establish what the description of eighteenth-century and early nineteenth-century Africa as a cosmopolitan continent actually means. It will establish evidence that that was a period in which Africans were intensely engaged with people of other continents and yet retained an incredible diversity of social strategies and systems. This cosmopolitan period would end with the coming of European-style capitalism and colonialism in the late nineteenth century, which together destroyed this diversity and imposed instead a near-universal hierarchical system of governance and social rules.

There is no perfect way to talk about this period so that it would be perfectly familiar to eighteenth-century Africans and so that contemporary readers could also understand it with total accuracy. For example, in our own society we understand state, economy, and religion as separate categories, but most eighteenth-century Africans seem to have seen them as deeply overlapping. Similarly, this chapter presents commonly understood English terms like clan" that are helpful but not precisely analogous to what Bugandans or Asante citizens of the period would have understood. However, when carefully contextualized these are the terms that best fit the dual needs of explaining African societies from their own perspectives and translating them for a contemporary audience.

Most of this chapter is engaged with understanding the social organization and worldviews of specific societies: the emerging kingdom of Buganda in the highlands of eastern Africa, the physical and spirit worlds of the Xhosa near the southern edge of the continent, the descent groups and entrepreneurial opportunities that supported the Asante Confederation in what is today Ghana, the balancing act

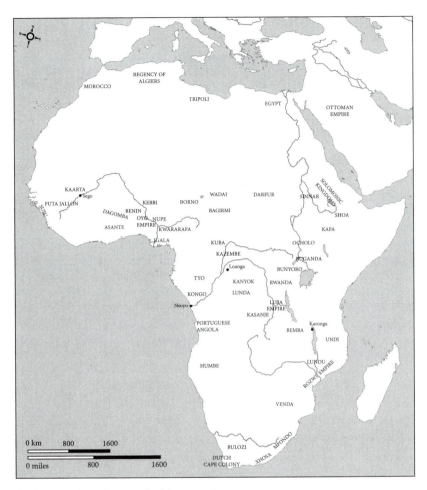

MAP 1   Political map of Africa, c. 1750

of gender and status that bound together the decentralized communities of the Igbo-speakers to their east, and the interwoven peasant and aristocratic communities that made up the Kongo state in Central Africa. The final section of this chapter is an in-depth study of documents from a religious and political movement in Kongo. These documents, interpreted by historian John Thornton, help us to understand the intellectual and emotional perspectives of the Kongolese as the eighteenth century began.

SPIRIT POWER AND STATE POWER IN BUGANDA

Human history is deeply embedded in the Great Lakes region of Africa. Stretching from what is today western Kenya and Uganda down through Tanzania to Malawi, this region includes the Great Rift Valley, which was home to many of our early human ancestors and has been a meeting place for various groups of humans ever since. The ancestors of the current population in the region, for example, included speakers of at least three major human language groups: the Niger-Congo family of languages (including the Bantu group of languages), the Nilo-Saharan family, and an older but no longer existing set of languages spoken by hunter-gatherers who occupied the region prior to the arrival of the other groups.

Despite this diversity, however, identity in the Great Lakes region has rarely been determined by language or other simple markers of ethnicity. Instead, the inhabitants of this area have developed complex, interwoven structures to ensure stability and try to enhance their survival and wealth. Two examples of these are the "clan" and "kingdom" structures developed by Ganda society in the region to the north of Lake Victoria Nyanza, the world's second-largest lake in terms of surface area.

The older of these two institutions is the clan. Unlike hierarchical political structures in which power is exerted vertically by superior individuals or groups upon inferiors, the clan acts as a horizontal power structure in which establishing relationships with equals allows an individual or group to become powerful. The BaGanda (Ganda people) today explicitly speak of the clans as large families, each with its own animal totem—the leopard, the civet cat, and the lungfish are some examples. This has led historians and anthropologists to largely accept the outward formulation of clans as groups of blood kin descended from a common ancestor. The BaGanda also tend to speak of some clans as representing a group of indigenous residents, with other clans representing waves of immigrants who arrived each in their own turn, and many scholars have accepted this understanding as well.

In fact, however, the clans probably represent a much more complex process of social formation. Historical anthropologist Neil Kodesh spent many years working with BaGanda, and he believes that clans had their origins before the fourteenth century as local spirit-possession cults, each with its own shrine and group of mediums, or interpreters. In the fifteenth and sixteenth centuries, development of techniques for cultivating bananas and plantains and a resulting jump in population led to competition for resources, especially arable land. This in turn created new tensions: the need for mutual self-defense against invaders who wished to seize land and contests to determine who would inherit land. At the same time, it created new opportunities for social and political organization as the increase in calorie yields allowed for the development of groups of religious and technological specialists who did not have to spend all of their time growing food.

In the midst of this tumult, the inhabitants of this region adapted their spirit cults into a political tool. The mediums and the spirits they represented became means for resolving conflict and healing rifts within the communities. Successful spirits—those whose clans thrived—were often adopted by people from outside the community. This in turn encouraged the spirits and their interpreters or priests to become mobile, moving among many different shrines across wide regions. This extended community, stretched widely, needed a new way to stay unified, and the spirits provided this not only by resolving problems but also by offering a story that explained why all its members should stick together. The result was that the community became a clan, with a set of stories about shared ancestors and values that may or may not have been accurate. By the early eighteenth century, the BaGanda therefore organized themselves as members of many clans, each cemented together by mobile mediums, networks of shrines, and myths about shared ancestry.

The big political change that emerged within the region in the late seventeenth and early eighteenth centuries was the rise of a state that brought the clans together. This state was (and still is) known as Buganda (the Ganda kingdom). There had been kingdoms in this region before, including a large state known as Bunyoro that continued as Buganda's neighbor. In most of these, however, the kingdom was really one royal clan ruling over other clans. Buganda was something different. While its early *kabaka* (kings) such as Kateregga and Jjunju used the language and ideas of clanship to justify their rule, they also developed new, royal ideologies that included marriage among many different clans. This meant that rather than acting as a conquering clan and angering all the other clans, the rulers tried to entice the local clans into seeing advantages to participating in the state.

The royal ideology of the Buganda state centered upon convincing the various clans to see the kingdom as a way to advance their own power, wealth, and stability. Thus the kings and their advisers developed a series of rituals and stories that brought the clan together with the state. For example, the main ceremonies marking the elevation of a king or preparing the state for battle required the presence of representatives from many clans, each with his or her own role. Similarly, the mythical ancestors of major clans were elevated to the status of national ancestors by being given new stories as to how they helped to forge the Buganda state. This is probably true of the alleged "first king" of Buganda, Kintu, who may have been an entirely mythical ancestor of a particular clan before becoming the BaGanda national father.

Of course, the kings sometimes clashed politically with the elders and spirit mediums who ran the clans. Thus in the late eighteenth and nineteenth centuries, for example, some rulers tried to appoint chiefs to run newly conquered territories rather than just incorporating their clans into the clan structure of the state. These chiefs were loyal to the king and helped to elevate his power. Often, however, these attempts to solidify royal power were unsuccessful, and the various clans managed to reassert their ability to rein in and limit the power of the kings. At the same time, new groups joined the kingdom and were assimilated into this system both by joining existing clans and by creating new clans of their own that were integrated into the politics of the nation while their ancestral figures were given a place in the myth-history of the nation. Thus well into the nineteenth century, political power in the kingdom was balanced between the *kabaka* and his court on the one hand and clan leaderships on the other. While sometimes causing internal conflict, this balance generally ensured that nobody could get too powerful, that the state remained unified, and that the people could get about on their daily business of pursuing survival, prosperity, and happiness. It also made it possible for new groups—whether annexed or voluntarily attached by migration or negotiation—to become part of the nation. In this sense, Buganda managed to be both cosmopolitan and unified at the same time.

XHOSA WORLDS: HOMESTEAD, NEIGHBORHOOD, KINGDOM, ANCESTORS

The structures of the BaGandan clans and kingdom were just one strategy pursued by African communities to pursue stability and prosperity in a cosmopolitan setting. Another example comes from the very southern tip of Africa, where communities from two languages groups—the Khoisan family and the Nguni group of the Bantu family—intermingled for centuries prior to the 1600s and jointly constructed a society that came to be known as the Xhosa (Xhosa people). Because the Xhosa bordered upon relatively sparsely populated regions in this period, theirs was an expansion-oriented society that slowly integrated large areas of land and many local populations.

In the seventeenth century, Xhosa society enjoyed a mix of technologies and social structures that reflected this melding of cultures. IsiXhosa (the Xhosa language) is a member of the Bantu language group related to those found across the trunk of Africa, but it borrows not only words but also sounds from Khoisan languages indigenous to southern Africa. Both many Khoisan-speaking and Bantu-speaking groups in this region shared a number of cultural values, including a focus on cattle as an economic commodity and a social good. Cattle were not only living wealth but also the keys to the reproduction and expansion of the family or community. They could be exchanged for other foodstuffs, used for milk or less often meat, given to others as part of an alliance or even in exchange for wives. They could be slaughtered as messengers to communicate with the ancestors and in rituals that strengthened the community. As a result, they came to occupy the imagination of the Xhosa. Poetry and other cultural expressions arose to describe the shape and virtues of bulls and cows, and their owners developed close bonds with them, at times even decorating their bodies.

Cattle were generally owned by men, and, although they remained relatively evenly distributed across Xhosa society in the seventeenth century, important men could own hundreds or even thousands. These important or senior men lived in homesteads with their families—wives and unmarried children—and sometimes other related or unrelated dependents. Their homesteads were the central economic and social unit of society, and labor was divided within them by the gender and age of their members. Xhosa homesteads were by the early eighteenth century spread across the countryside of what is today the Eastern Cape province of South Africa and somewhat beyond. They were further organized into neighborhoods, each of which was led by a chiefly family. Chiefs passed on their authority within their families, although new chiefs had to be approved by the community.

Like the BaGanda, the Xhosa understood themselves as organized into clans, although these were not politically very powerful. Also like the BaGanda, each clan claimed a particular origin from a single Bantu-speaking or Khoisan-speaking ancestor, although in fact it is likely that all clans were a mix of both. Clans did play a role in marriage, since there were ritual prohibitions against marrying within the clan. Moreover, because they were spread across wide regions, they functioned to protect cattle from disease, predation, or warfare. Men could and often did place several of their cows and bulls with distant clan members for periods of time, thus ensuring that not all their eggs were in one basket (or cattle in one field!).

Chieftaincy was politically more important than the clan in the eighteenth century and was intricately tied in to the age-grade system. Age-grades were institutions by which all the members of a neighborhood (or chieftaincy) who were of a similar age were initiated into adulthood together. In most cases, this was a relatively minor ritual. However, when the son of a chief came of age, it could be quite important. In order to avoid conflict, a chief's sons usually left for new territories upon coming of age. This was the process by which Xhosa society expanded.

Boys initiated into manhood alongside the sons of a chief became his first councillors, and therefore fathers would often hold back or try to advance their sons' initiations to match those of their chief's sons. Sometime later, the young chief and his councillors and other followers would usually depart for the new territory. These territories, however, were often already occupied—frequently by Khoisan-speakers. The new arrivals would at times have to fight, marry, or otherwise integrate the local population. Through this process, the locals would over time become assimilated into Xhosa society, although sometimes reshaping Xhosa society to their own needs in turn.

By the eighteenth century, the Xhosa had also developed the overarching political structure of a kingdom that played some role in expansion and other processes. However, the Xhosa kingdom was relatively week. The *inkosi* (monarch) confirmed new chiefs in their positions and also had certain powers to adjudicate disputes, especially in terms of who controlled land, as well as to declare war. However, he also had little authority over his chiefs. Rather, he was forced to consult with them before making most decisions. Thus he was frequently imagined as the "oldest brother" among the chiefs rather than a superior individual, and he had no standing bureaucracy or royal army. Similarly, both the king and chiefs were restricted in their ability to control commoners, especially important household heads. For example, household heads had full rights to the land they worked so long as they discharged certain ritual obligations like the sharing of some crops and hunted animals with their chiefs. Wealthy commoners also held important positions as councillors to both chiefs and kings and could withhold their support if they felt they were being badly treated. In the same way, although commoners had to pay taxes and tributes to their chiefs and to the king, they could protest unfair taxation.

This balance of power and authority between chiefs, kings, and commoners was reflected in the ways in which isiXhosa-speakers approached spirituality and religion. On the one hand, spiritual practices contributed to the stability of the state. Chiefs affirmed their loyalty to kings by acknowledging their power to determine when certain crops could be harvested, for example, and commoners acknowledged the authority of chiefs by obeying rules as to who could speak to the chief and when. These rules were perceived as being part of the way in which ancestors and spirits determined the order of the world. Conversely, however, for every ritual of hierarchy there were specific exceptions. For example, when a new chief was being chosen, elderly commoners could use the moment to insult him, thus reminding him that he was still a member of society rather than being above the rules.

Interfacing with the world of spirits and ancestors was an important part of the lives of the seventeenth-century Xhosa and was partly carried out through diviners. Some diviners were attached to chiefs or kings, but most were independent. People turned to diviners in times of trouble to determine what had gone wrong. In general, the Xhosa worldview was one in which failures were the result either of some malevolent person or of a failure to treat the ancestors well and to listen to their advice. Diviners could determine these problems, since they were attuned to the world of the ancestors and spirits and could receive advice or instructions directly from them. However, they could not operate simply on their own individual authority. Diviners were initiated and regulated by a society or guild. This was important because diviners wielded great power in identifying who within society was acting as a malevolent force or "witch." They could abuse this power by, for example, designating a wealthy commoner as a witch in order to allow a chief to seize his or her property. The guild was supposed to limit the chance of this abuse by regulating the diviners and, if necessary, investigating them.

Together, these institutions helped to shape the everyday lives of Xhosa. Of course, it is important not to try to reduce their life experiences to these few categories. Individuals interacted within the institutions of Xhosa society in various ways and made individual decisions.

There was apparently some diversity of belief, for example, between those who followed a more naturalistic view of earth and water spirits and others who focused more on ancestors as spiritual guides. Also, we must recognize that Xhosa shared a great many of their views and social institutions with neighboring people like independent Khoisan communities and other Bantu-speakers, and that their identify was therefore fluid rather than closed. This was a basic feature of their cosmopolitan social organization, and it complicates any attempt at a simplified understanding of their lives and worldviews. Nevertheless, understanding the ways in which they organized their society gives us our first insights into how they understood and interacted with the world in which they lived.

MATRICLANS AND ENTREPRENEURS IN THE MAKING OF THE ASANTE STATE

Like the BaGanda and Xhosa, the Akan-speaking people who formed the bulk of the population of the Asante Confederation in the early eighteenth century organized themselves through an institution of clans. For the inhabitants of Asante, these were called *abusua* and were "matriclans," meaning that membership in a particular *abusua* was based on descent from the mother. Any individual within the society would normally be a member of his or her mother's clan rather than his or her father's.

The institution of the matriclan in this region probably dates back to the fourteenth century, when it evolved out of the need for the ancestors of the Asante to clear forests for use as fields. In the densely forested Pra River basin they inhabited, the clearing of new fields required enormous effort but only every five years or so, since each cleared field was usually fertile for that length of time before being abandoned to return to forest. Thus the ability to organize seasonal labor to clear a particular individual's fields was of great benefit, and the matriclan created a permanent pool of labor to work on different fields on a rotating basis. The matriclan also created a structure to assimilate strangers into the group through marriage, thus increasing the productivity of the family. Finally, it was an institution by which a group of people could collectively distribute land and manage disputes. At least initially, women were quite powerful in these matriclans, since they had the ability to assimilate outside men by marrying them.

At the same time, however, some members of Akan society found that the matriclan also had drawbacks. Because land and resources were communally owned through the *abusua* system, individual entrepreneurship was somewhat restricted. It was only the development of a long-distance trade in kola nuts in the sixteenth century and gold and slave trades in the seventeenth century that led to some individuals becoming wealthy, and also created the ambition for wealth among others. These ambitious entrepreneurs, finding insufficient room for individual landowning and property accumulation in the Akan heartland, thus began to set out for new areas and settled in them, often taking with them immediate members of their families and other dependents. Once they found a new place, they would build estates and frequently intermarry with the local population. Other settlers followed as well, and the original entrepreneurs and their families began to form a sort of nobility with the new settlers beneath them. Thus emerged the institution of chieftainship, the *ahenfo*, and the state, or *oman*. Through this process, male power seems to have surpassed female power, since the entrepreneurs-turned-chiefs were mostly men.

The process of settlement led to the creation of numerous independent Akan-speaking states. Any survey of these states around 1700 would see that they included many different models. At the edges of the forest—especially along the coast and near the savanna—small states were often organized around trading cities. In these communities, chiefs were often quite weak and merchants powerful. This was true, for example, of the group of Akan states known as the Fante in the region that is now the central coast of Ghana. To the east of the Fante states, in an area where Akan-speakers had absorbed many distinct preexisting communities, the patrilineal clan structure of these groups sometimes replaced matrilineal clans. In the heartland of the Akan-speaking territories, however, large centralized states jostled for power. Right around 1700, a state emerged that would come to occupy most of what is today Ghana—the state of Asante.

Asante began as a relatively weak state dependent on another, neighboring state called Denkyira. The first ruler of an independent Asante, Osei Tutu, had spent time both in the royal court of Denkyira and in a neighboring state called Akwamu, to which he fled as a young man, allegedly following a dalliance with the sister of the king of Denkyira. It was Osei Tutu who led a war of independence against Denkyira, aided by divisions within Denkyira and the support of a religious leader named Okomfo Anokye. Following the war, around

1701, Osei Tutu's Asante and four allied states formed a confederation with a set of rules that carefully balanced the power of various chiefs and rulers. At the head of the state were Osei Tutu and his successors, although the other ruling families were guaranteed certain rights and positions. In order to bind the states together, Osei Tutu and Anokye helped to promote a national origin myth represented by the "golden stool," a throne that supposedly descended from heaven, and an annual festival in which each of the rulers of the provinces and their chiefs pledged loyalty to the Asante king (or *Asantehene*). This act also was believed to renew the health and fertility of the soil and people, thus linking the health of the king to the prosperity of the greater populace.

However, the state was only one contender for the people's attention and loyalties in this region. Akan-speakers, like the majority inhabitants of Asante, were also engaged in a relationship with both the material world of the forest and the nonmaterial world hidden within it. In the eighteenth century, Asante both feared and appreciated the forest around them. On the one hand, the forest was a place of disorder where spirits and monsters could threaten travelers. On the other hand, its fertility could be harnessed and its spirits ordered to help people. In previous periods, it had been thought that women were most able to do this, but by the eighteenth century most Asante believed that male elders were best able to communicate with the spirit world.

Nor were the forest spirits the only nonmaterial entities of importance. Most Asante believed they could communicate with personal spirits who were tied to their ancestors. At the same time, they generally worshiped an all-powerful god, Onyame. Priests like Anokye were especially powerful in communicating with Onyame, and the Asante kings thus carefully sought alliances with them in order to turn the king into a powerful moral and religious figure. By the end of the eighteenth century, it was commonly believed that the king was able to intercede on behalf of his people with Onyame. At the same time, religious minorities, including Muslims, were allowed to pursue their own styles of worship and beliefs.

The Asante kings were also closely involved in the growing economy that funded the state's expansion. Asante social values generally embraced the accumulation of wealth by individuals, matriclans, and even the state. Eighteenth-century Asante had a large economy with some goods funneled into markets for local production and others—especially kola and gold—sent long distances. The growth of an Atlantic market for slaves also helped propel the state to expand northward into the interior of West Africa, where Asante forces conquered many non-Akan peoples. In general, these new provinces were left out of the power-sharing structure of the Asante state but were largely allowed to rule themselves so long as they provided tribute in the form of slaves and other goods to the Asante royal court.

Because of its size and the nature of its rule of the periphery provinces, the Asante state is sometimes called an "empire" and sometimes a "confederation." Both terms are of some use in understanding the ways in which the Asante organized their society. At its heart, Asante society was organized as a network of power shared by kings and their royal officials, the elders of matriclans, and independent chiefly office-holders. These individuals represented various confederated groups willingly tying themselves to the throne through agreements that were ritually renewed every year. Most Asante citizens, represented by these leaders, had relative freedom on a day-to-day basis, although they also acknowledged their obligations to their clan, chiefs, kings, ancestors, and god. Moreover, Asante society was cosmopolitan in that it found places for both local and immigrant Muslims and non-Akan peoples. However, these individuals were not always regarded as full citizens, especially if they came from the outer provinces of the state. In this respect, the Asante state acted as an empire as well as a confederation.

TITLES AND LINEAGES IN IGBO-SPEAKING SOCIETIES

Not all African peoples responded to the challenges and opportunities of their environments by organizing themselves into large states. The communities of the Niger River delta, for example, though surrounded by many centralized and hierarchical states, nevertheless supported a number of alternate social systems in the eighteenth century. Many of these took the form of crosscutting associations that wove people together in webs of interaction but without establishing governments per se. Three principal associations shaped the lives of most Igbo-speakers in the eighteenth century. The first was the sodality—sisterhoods and brotherhoods of people raised to "noble" rank. The second was the extended family. The third was the guild or professional association. Exactly how each of these associations worked, however, varied across the region. In each community, guilds could be weak or strong, sodalities could be secret or open, and families could be organized along patrilineal (membership passed down through the father) or matrilineal (membership passed down through the mother) lines.

Usually, the lineage was the most prominent association to which an individual belonged. Extended family structures among Igbo-speakers did not ordinarily function politically in the way clans operated in Buganda, although they did tie people together to each other and to a shared set of mythical or real ancestors. They also played a distinct role in the governance of community activities, as lineage elders sometimes congregated to make decisions. Groups of lineages were also believed to be "related" to each other, with some lineages seen as being more important or "senior," and others as junior. Often, several lineages would have obligations toward each other, although these were usually ritual rather than any real transfer of wealth or exercise of authority.

Whereas just about everyone other than the very lowest-status inhabitants belonged to lineages, only a small percentage of Igbo-speaking adults could become members of the various sodalities within the region. Membership was bestowed on individuals who were very successful, often having proved their virtues through the accumulation of wealth in the form of yams or other commodities. Men and women who became members of these sodalities were considered to be "titled" or "noble," although this did not mean that they could command others. In fact, one of the roles of the sodalities seems to have been to redistribute wealth from successful individuals to the wider community, since nobles were responsible for providing feasts at annual religious ceremonies (like the yam festival) or life-cycle rituals such as child naming, marriage, and funerals.

Probably the least well-known and significant associations were the professional guilds, for example, smiths and leatherworkers, which could exert a certain amount of power in specific ritual and economic areas involving their crafts. In the case of these two crafts, the profession was often hereditary and believed to involve certain mystical or spiritual properties. For this reason, the metalworking and leatherworking guilds were in many cases socially distinct from other groups in society and even confined to certain districts and sections of towns.

All these associations contributed to the decentralized nature of Igbo society. Yet while decentralized, large portions of the Igbo-speaking community could nevertheless be called together by a number of generally acknowledged institutions whose power rose and waned over long periods. The most important of these were oracles maintained by diviners who had the ability to communicate with the world of the ancestors. Two of the most significant oracles were Agbala and Ibini Okpube. They were seen as existing at the junction of spiritual and human existence and were therefore keys to the process by which the Igbo-speakers' worldview was maintained and at times changed. In the eighteenth century, the dominant expression of this worldview seems to have been the idea of "balance." Through this value, individual achievement was important, but it should be balanced by the good of the association, whether it be community, lineage, sodality, or guild. Thus equality of opportunity was to be balanced with the promotion of competition. Similarly, the world of the ancestors was to be balanced with the world of the living. So long as the world was in balance, the social structure and the individual would thrive. By extension, if a group or individual suffered misfortune, it was probably because the balance had been disturbed somehow and needed to be redressed. Through the oracles or individual diviners, these problems could be divined and solutions negotiated between the ancestors and the living. Often, this was done publicly or at least in the presence of the kin group, the community, or the sodality.

Seemingly important rules of the community or other association could be contravened if necessary to keep some balance. This can be demonstrated by attitudes toward gender. It is accurate to say, for example, that there was a division of labor and rights between men and women. However, if a man did not have a son, it was possible in many cases for him to elevate his daughter to be a "male daughter," essentially to function as a son in terms of labor and inheritance and thus to redress the imbalance caused by the lack of a son. Similarly, one way an individual could accumulate wealth and prestige was through having many wives, since women carried out much of the agricultural labor. Women, however, could not acquire wives and thus might have been excluded from this pathway to wealth. But there was a loophole. Some wealthy single women could acquire other, often enslaved women and "marry" them. In this case, the wealthy women became known as "husbands" and had the same rights vis-à-vis their wives as a man had toward his.

Thus eighteenth-century Igbo society serves as an example of the fact that in Africa, as elsewhere, society was built up of both rules and exceptions, shared experiences and individual aspirations. However, Igbo society was particularly cosmopolitan in that its interlocking web of internal associations and lack of centralization allowed for a great diversity of individual life experiences and created many places at which immigrants and locally born members of society could attach themselves and experiment with social and cultural conceptions as well as economic projects.

TUNIS UNDER THE BEYS

Igbo-speaking societies could perhaps be expected to be diverse and rather loose, since there was no great overarching state structure to control them. But what about African societies that were part of centralized empires?

The largest state in Africa at the beginning of the eighteenth century was the Turkic Ottoman Empire, which by the end of the sixteenth century had occupied Egypt and much of the Mediterranean seaboard of the continent (aside from Morocco, which remained independent). The territory that constitutes Tunisia today was the westernmost province of this empire. Ottoman forces had seized this territory in response to the expansion of Spain, and both international trade and war were facts of life for its inhabitants in the eighteenth century. It might be expected that a vast empire like that of the Ottoman sultans would rule with a rigid hand, carefully controlling all aspects of society. In fact, however, Tunisians' life experiences under Ottoman rule were varied and in many cases only vaguely affected by Ottoman influence and laws.

This was the case even in the city of Tunis, capital of the Ottoman province of Tunisia. Tunis was even then a very old city, ruled in turn by Carthage, Rome, Berber-speaking peoples from the North African interior, the great Muslim caliphates, and local dynasties. In 1574, the city was captured by Ottoman forces during a conflict that drew in Spain and a number of other Mediterranean polities. It would remain technically an Ottoman province until 1881.

Like other African societies of the period, eighteenth-century society in Tunis was constructed from a number of interlocking identity groups and institutions. At the top of the state was the imperial pasha, or bey, a Turkic official who ruled the province, and a body of other soldiers and administrators sent out by the Ottoman regime. But there were also powerful local families known as the *khassa*. Composed of both merchants and Islamic scholars, these families were not technically nobles but instead held their authority by virtue of their religious learning and their wealth.

Beneath these two elites were large and diverse communities that occupied separate but overlapping quarters of the city. The largest were the Islamic communities, including the Malikites (indigenous Tunisians), Hanafites (largely Turkish immigrants), and Andalusians (Muslims from Spain). There were also religious minorities such as Christians and Jews and small communities of normally nomadic or rural Muslims such as Berbers and Bedouin. Each of these groups was largely self-governing on a day-to-day basis. In fact, most issues were resolved at the level of the neighborhood. This led to a generally decentralized civic life. Another force for decentralization was the guilds. Tunis was a highly commercial city linked in to Mediterranean and trans-Saharan trade routes. The city produced many goods, including intricate leatherwork and metalwork. This production was governed through a system of professional guilds whose members largely supervised themselves. In some cases, guild leaders even exercised the functions of judges. Technically, this authority was granted them by the bey, but in fact they were largely independent.

Given this decentralization, what was it that bound the diverse inhabitants of this city together and rendered it governable? In the eighteenth century, the main factor was the opportunistic cosmopolitanism of the beys. These imperial governors relied on the many communities for both tax funds and political support. Recognizing this, they tried to make themselves patrons of all of these groups. Politically, the Hanafite and Malakite Muslim communities were the most important. Thus, the beys tried to please both communities by appointing members of each to lucrative positions such as collecting taxes. They also donated to mosques and religious orders representing both groups and portrayed themselves as being descended from marriages between generations of Turkic (Hanafite) officials and Tunisian (Malakite) women. Finally, they gave important positions and favors to prominent local *khassa* families, making them in turn dependent on the state, yet at the same time still gave a great deal of authority to Turkic-speaking army officers from the Ottoman heartland.

Perhaps most important, the beys largely stayed out of the internal business of the various groups they ruled. Their rule was generally very superficial and did not intrude on the day-to-day activities of the many guilds and identity groups in the capital. Indeed, they restricted themselves to appointing a few necessary bureaucrats and agents, maintaining a military force loyal to them against internal challenges and external threats, and collecting enough money to run the military and fund their own luxury. Otherwise, they largely left the city's groups to their own devices.

As a result, the cosmopolitan society of Tunis functioned in a relatively decentralized but effective way. It remained economically successful in this period, with a great deal of unregulated cottage industry (weaving, pottery, perfumes, jewelry, shoemaking). Religious groups and guilds remained largely self-adjudicating. Outside of the city, various towns and communities were largely run by their own elites. Admittedly, this strategy had its limitations. For example, it was difficult to mobilize the entire state for large projects. For example, the eighteenth-century beys found it difficult to unify the state when outside threats emerged, as we will see. However, it was also a very successful strategy for maintaining peace and stability in a volatile, diverse region in which Europeans, Asians, and Africans shared both trade and war.

REINING IN GREED AND ANARCHY IN BAKONGO AND JAGA STATE AND SOCIETY

The Mediterranean coast was not the only region in which Africans interacted intensively with people from other continents in the eighteenth century. As I discuss in the next chapter, this was a period of extensive transcontinental trade and interaction for Africans living along the Atlantic coast, in the seaboards bordering the Red Sea and Indian Ocean, and even at the southern tip of the continent. One of several such regions was the Central African state of Kongo.

Prior to the eighteenth century, Kongo was a kingdom of many provinces surrounded by numerous other kingdoms, but it also had a rather unique social and economic situation. In fact, Kongo could be said to have been two loosely interwoven societies existing in a single territory. The first of these was a rural peasantry that lived in small communities of a few households producing goods along the lines of a sexual division of labor—women produced most of the foodstuffs, and men specialized in manufacturing consumer goods. Each of these communities functioned as a sort of "republic." The households shared their products, passing some on to their selected leaders—a group of elders and a small number of *kitomi*, or religious leaders. These groups offered political and religious guidance and protection, but their lives differed little from those of other members of the community.

The second society was made up of a number of towns, or *mbanza*, the largest of which was São Salvador (also known as Mbanza Kongo), which at its height may have held 60,000 people. The towns were ruled by a class of nobles, the *mani*, who relied for most of their goods on a class of serfs. The nobility owned the land around the big towns and managed groups of these laborers who owed them "rent" in labor but otherwise had considerable freedom.

The two societies were loosely connected through the payment of "rent" by rural peoples to the nobility of the towns in the form of metal, bark cloth, wild animal products, shells, and some foodstuffs. Some rural villages specialized in particular local products. Other than this connection and a tenuous political unity, however, they were two worlds that remained largely separate.

In the seventeenth century, the political intersection of the two Kongolese societies was vested in the state. The monarchy was quite large and well established, comprising a king and his court—including bureaucrats, judges, and personal servants who were often influential men and women. The king managed the *mbanza* by sending nobles out to administer them. However, these nobles did not get permanent title to the towns but rather acted merely as temporary administrators.

The city of Mbanza Kongo, c. 1700. This view includes the king's Palace, Christian churches, and the Portuguese fort.

Their main job was to make sure that the towns remained stable and secure and to extract rent from the rural areas of the provinces. They seem to have been motivated largely by a desire to be seen as successful administrators and then to be called back to the royal court where power was located and life was easy.

The worldview of the Kongolese nobility embraced personal accumulation and power, as might have been expected of a society divided by class such as theirs. Yet in general, they held back from extracting too much wealth from the peasants, who tended in fact to live relatively long and prosperous lives compared, for example, with many European peasants of the period. What was it that protected the poor in this way? The answer seems to be that the Kongolese developed a philosophy of life that governed their economic transactions as well as their daily practices. At the center of the early eighteenth-century Kongolese worldview was a sense of morality in which greed was seen as a sign of witchcraft, necessitating revolt and other punishments for witches, including overly greedy nobles. This moral system was tied in to the dominant Kongolese spiritual system. The *kitomi*, aided in rural areas by the *nganga* (a class of spiritual diviners), managed this system of values and helped people to determine the cause of individual or community-wide problems. The *kitomi* were especially important because they did this publicly. Often, their function was to identify for society which individuals had been overly greedy, and to publicly warn them to stop. The arrival of Catholic priests in the sixteenth century did not change this, since the Kongolese generally saw them as just another type of *nganga* or *kitomi*. While there was a period in which the Catholic missionaries and indigenous religious individuals called each other witches, in general they coexisted relatively successfully.

As we can see, the Kongo lived in a highly ordered world in which community prosperity generally trumped individual aspiration. Many of their neighboring states and societies had similar emphases on communal economics and ethics, although their systems were not the same. In the seventeenth century, however, the BaKongo moral system began to be challenged in several ways. The main challenge came from the Atlantic slave trade, which included violence that broke apart communities and examples of enormous greed as European slave traders and African slavers destroyed local societies for personal enrichment. What was the impact of this process on Africans?

One answer can be seen in the actions of the Jaga (sometimes called Imbangala) in this period. The Jaga are often depicted by the inhabitants of West-Central African states in this period as barbarian invaders from the interior. In fact, however, they were probably the survivors of societies that had been repeatedly attacked by slave raiders. Jaga society was highly mobile and dedicated to war. Columns of Jaga were organized into army units, preying upon whatever communities they found and destroying whatever they could not take with them. In fact, they appear in many cases to have killed their own children rather than carrying them with them. How can this very different type of existence be explained? Anthropologist and historian Jan Vansina has suggested that the Jaga were refugees from societies like Kongo that had once been in balance, but where the Atlantic slave trade had caused such out-of-control greed that the entire social and belief system had been destroyed and, in many cases, their children kidnapped for export. The Jaga had been victims but now chose to be victims no more. By traveling around without possessions or children, they no longer had anything that could be taken from them. At the same time, by raiding the larger states, they were attacking the nobles whom they felt had broken the moral code by engaging in slave trading. In that way, the Jaga can be seen as a revolt of the "have-nots" against the "haves."

Beatriz as Saint Anthony

The emergence of the Jaga was one symptom of the breakdown of societies in West-Central Africa during the period of the Atlantic slave trade. The Kongolese state itself, however, withstood such a collapse until the mid–seventeenth century. When its downfall came, it was a result of several factors. First, beginning in the 1640s, the *mani Kongo* (king of Kongo), Garcia II, fell into a series of disputes with Catholic missionaries, some of whom were persecuting local religious leaders. Although Garcia in fact sympathized personally with the missionaries, he recognized that their actions had aggravated many of the rural Kongolese, who had turned to local religious movements like the *kimpasi* sect in response. The missionaries in turn complained of this response to the Portuguese, who controlled the nearby territory of Luanda. They were joined by Portuguese merchants who were angry that the Kongolese were trading with other Europeans. The result was a Portuguese invasion of Kongo in 1665. The Portuguese were also aided by a number of Jaga mercenaries. This war began the slow decline of the state. In the 1670s, rival nobles sought to be selected as the new king, and in 1678 the capital city was sacked in a war between several of them.

The destruction of São Salvador destroyed the carefully balanced dual urban-rural system of the Kongo state. Without a royal court and a king, there was no system to apportion nobles to the provinces and no order to bring them back to retire in comfort to the capital city. Instead, the nobles began to settle permanently in the provinces as warlords, fighting against each other for advantage. The results for the peasants of the rural areas appeared only gradually but were terrible. Faced with conscription into the armies of the warlords and higher tax burdens to pay for the wars, the peasant communities rapidly lost both wealth and population.

By the first years of the eighteenth century, the people of the various Kongolese provinces were disheartened and suffering. Thus, they eagerly embraced an opportunity to unify the kingdom and restore the prosperity and peace of earlier eras. This opportunity came in the form of Dona Beatriz Kimpa Vita, a woman who claimed to be the reincarnation of Saint Anthony, whom she asserted had been Kongolese.

The life of Dona Beatriz is useful for us because it tells us something about the emotions and thinking of the Kongolese in this period. She herself was born a low-level noblewoman in the capital of one of the aspirants to the throne. As a young woman, she was trained to be an *nganga*, and specifically to help divine the causes of problems affecting wider society. She was also been initiated into the *kimpasi* society, a religious community of like-minded *ngangas*. However, she also had training in Catholic rites. She brought all these influences together in the religious movement she created and its particular understanding of power and righteousness. First, like other *kimpasi* society leaders before her, she rejected the special authority of the European Catholic priests, arguing that in fact the Kongolese could determine the gospel themselves. Yet she also embraced some aspects of Catholicism. In fact, she asserted that the church had been founded in Kongo first, and that not only Saint Anthony but also Saint Francis were Kongolese. Even Jesus she believed to have been born in São Salvador, which city she believed was Jerusalem and which she was committed to refounding. She promised her followers that the resettlement of that city would lead to a reunification of the kingdom and a new era of wealth, and she called upon the nobility to turn their back on warfare and greed and return to the balance of the period prior to the civil wars.

Historian John K. Thornton has pointed out that the perspective of Beatriz Kimpa Vita and her followers is demonstrated in her reworking of the Catholic Salve Regina (Hail, Holy Queen) prayer into a new prayer, the Salve Antonio (Hail, Saint Anthony):

> Salve you say and you do not know why. Salve you recite and you do not know why. Salve you beat and you do not know why. God wants the intention, it is the intention that God takes. Baptism serves nothing, it is the intention that God takes. Confession serves nothing, it is the intention that God takes. Prayer serves nothing, it is the intention that God wants. The mother with her son on her knees. If there

had not been St. Anthony what would they have done? St. Anthony is the merciful one. St. Anthony is our remedy. St. Anthony is the restorer of the kingdom of Kongo. St. Anthony is the comforter of the kingdom of Heaven. St. Anthony is the door to Heaven. St. Anthony holds the keys to Heaven. St. Anthony is above the Angels and the Virgin Mary. St. Anthony is the second God. [216]

As Thornton points out, this prayer is not much like the original but rather functions as a critique that asserts a particularly Kongolese understanding of the world. First, it rejects the authority of the European missionaries by suggesting that their prayer (Salve) has no special power. Instead, it suggests that the *intention* of the individual is what matters. This very much reflects the Kongolese belief in malevolent or benevolent forces influencing the lives of people, and the assertion that *nganga* like Beatriz Kimpa Vita could determine the intent with which people acted. The Salve Antonio also elevates the (Kongolese) Saint Anthony to a position equal to God and suggests that he was the redeemer not only of individuals but of the whole country. It promises that he would exhibit mercy upon the Kongolese people by restoring the state and bringing balance back to society. In this way Saint Anthony was much like an ancestor figure, but one who had been reincarnated in Beatriz Kimpa Vita and thus was very much alive.

Yet this restoration was not just meant to be literary. Beatriz and her followers also tried to put the revival of the kingdom and their society into motion by physically moving to the abandoned capital of São Salvador and then calling on the warlords to meet and unify the kingdom. In May 1706, however, Beatriz was captured by enemies and sentenced to death by a council of priests and nobles. Ironically, her execution helped pave the way for a reunification of the state in 1709 under an alliance of the warlords who had opposed her and supported her execution. Nevertheless, this restored monarchy was extremely weak, and the standard of living for most Kongolese never recovered. Moreover, the violence that ended the civil wars resulted in the enslavement of thousands of Kongolese, including many of Beatriz's followers. I will pick up their story in the next chapter.

REFERENCES

Spirit Power and State Power in Buganda
Kiwanuka, M. S. M. Semakula. *A History of Buganda: From the Foundation of the Kingdom to 1900* (New York: Africana Publishing, 1972).

Kodesh, Neil. *Beyond the Royal Gaze: Clanship and Public Healing in Buganda* (Charlottesville: University of Virginia Press, 2010).

Xhosa Worlds: Homestead, Neighborhood, Kingdom, Ancestors
Mabona, Mongameli. *Diviners and Prophets among the Xhosa (1593–1856): A Study in Xhosa Cultural History* (Münster: Lit Verlag, 2004).

Pieres, J. B. *The House of Phalo* (Johannesburg: Ravan Press, 1981).

Matriclans and Entrepreneurs in the Making of the Asante State
Akyeampong, Emmanuel, and Pashington Obeng. "Spirituality, Gender, and Power in Asante History." *International Journal of African Historical Studies* 28 (1995): 481–508.

Wilks, Ivor. *Forests of Gold: Essays on the Akan and the Kingdom of Asante* (Athens: Ohio University Press, 1993).

Titles and Lineages in Igbo-Speaking Societies
Amadiume, Ifi. *Male Daughters, Female Husbands: Gender and Sex in an African Society* (London: Zed Books, 1987).

Uchendu, Victor Chikezie. "Ezi Na Ulo: The Extended Family in Igbo Civilization." *Dialectical Anthropology* 31 (2007): 167–219.

Imperial Tunis
Abun-Nasr, Jamil. "The Tunisian State in the Eighteenth Century." *Revue l'Occident musulman et de la Méditerranée* 33 (1982): 33–66.

Moalla, Asma. *The Regency of Tunis and the Ottoman Porte, 1777–1814* (London: Routledge, 2004).

Reining In Greed and Anarchy in BaKongo and Jaga State and Society
Thornton, John K. *The Kingdom of Kongo: Civil War and Transition, 1641–1718.* Madison: University of Wisconsin Press, 1983.

Vansina, Jan. *How Societies Are Born: Governance in West Central Africa before 1600.* Charlottesville, University of Virginia Press, 2004,.

Beatriz as Saint Anthony
Thornton, John K. *The Kongolese Saint Anthony: Dona Beatriz Kimpa Vita and the Antonian Movement, 1684–1706.* Cambridge: Cambridge University Press, 1998.

Most of the sources for Kongo for this period have not been reprinted in English but many are available in French in L. Jadin, "Le Congo et la Secte des Antoniens: Restuaration du Royaume sous Petro IV et la 'Saint-Antoine Congolais' (1695-1718)." *Bulletin l'Institute Historique Belge de Rome* 33 (1961): 411–615.

Global Africa in an Oceanic Era

AN OCEANIC ERA

The eighteenth and nineteenth centuries were an oceanic era in world history. This is true not so much because there was a major turning point in oceanic travel in this period, but rather an acceleration of the trading voyages across the Mediterranean Sea and the Indian Ocean that had been operating for thousands of years and the transatlantic voyages that had in the fifteenth century. In the 300 years preceding 1750, innovations in shipbuilding, food preservation, medicine, and the science of navigation had helped to connect the populations of the world's continents to a greater degree than ever before. By the late eighteenth century, therefore, the volume of oceanic trade, including routes involving Africa, was steadily rising. Moreover, after 1815 the dhows of the Indian Ocean, barques of the Mediterranean, and galleons of the Atlantic were joined by coal-powered steamships, further hastening the integration of the world. This oceanic integration had an enormous impact on coastal African societies and a less significant but still important effect on Africans of the interior.

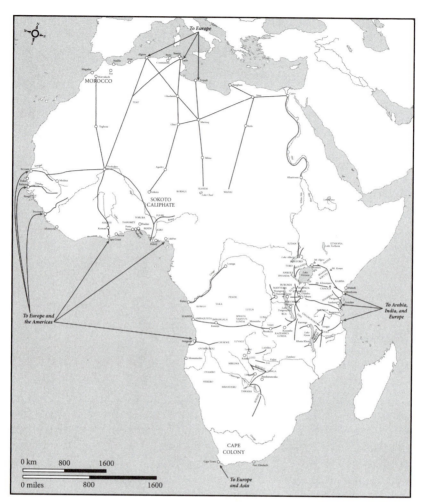

MAP 2 Key trade routes in and from Africa, nineteenth century

As a continent, Africa faces the rest of the world along three broad frontiers. In the north, the Mediterranean is little more than a pond between Europe, southwest Asia, and the North African societies of Egypt and the Maghreb. Records of voyages across this sea stretch back many thousands of years. To the east, the long coastline stretching from the Red Sea along the horn of Africa and down thousands of miles to the southern tip of the continent is connected by relatively predictable seasonal wind patterns to Arabia, India, the Indian Ocean islands, and Asian destinations beyond.

Voyages between these localities helped to create the cosmopolitan societies of the horn of Africa and the Swahili coast over many hundreds of years. In the west, the vast Atlantic separates Africa from the Americas, with few islands between. This was the last-breached frontier, first crossed by significant numbers of Europeans, Africans, and some Americans in the sixteenth century.

In 1750, all three frontiers were alive with commercial networks that connected Africans to other continents. The so-called Columbian exchange was in full effect as people, foodstuffs, diseases, species, and goods crossed the Atlantic between Europe, the Americas, and Africa. Trade in the Indian Ocean and Mediterranean was also increasing, if less dramatically. As a result, Africans living in this cosmopolitan age were keenly affected by many global events. Alongside the rise and fall of the Atlantic slave trade (see volume 1), some of most important of these were the Atlantic revolutions in France, Haiti, and the American colonies (1776–1820), the gradual retreat of the Ottoman Empire from some of its European and African provinces, the industrial revolution (discussed in chapter 4), and the rise of evangelical Christianity in Europe and Wahhabiyya in Arabia and elsewhere in the Muslim world (chapter 3).

In this chapter, I will look at the ways in which Africans sought to master the social and political transformations wrought by the gradually increasing interaction of this oceanic era. The first section focuses on the societies of the Maghreb and Egypt that bordered the Mediterranean and their interaction with Ottoman and European states and peoples. The second section looks at African participation in the major events and trends of the Atlantic world, including the development of creole societies on the continent and among societies with large proportions of African members in the Americas. Finally, the third section covers African participation in the Omani-Zanzibari, Portuguese, and to a lesser degree French and British trading networks in the Indian Ocean. In each case, we are particularly interested in the ways in which Africans' sense of their social and political selves shifted between 1750 and 1875. The case study for this chapter, the *Pate Chronicles*, illustrates this trend through a focus on evidence from a single East African city-state around 1800.

MEDITERRANEAN AFRICA

The history of the Mediterranean is one of interaction among the islands and coastal societies that border this slender, relatively calm body of water. On the European side, the fractured geography of islands and peninsulas contributed to the fragmentation of the coastline into numerous small states. Spanish unification was only achieved in the late fifteenth century, and around the same time France took possession of the Mediterranean provinces of Languedoc and Provence. Italy remained fragmented into numerous small states as late as 1871. On the African and Asiatic sides of the sea, by contrast, the long coastlines allowed for relatively large states and the domination of a single empire—the Ottoman sultanate—from the seventeenth to the nineteenth century. Only Morocco remained independent throughout this period, being too distant from the Ottoman capital of Constantinople and too self-sufficient to be successfully integrated.

Several broad trends contributed to the integration of the Mediterranean as a region by the eighteenth century. First, the relative stability of Ottoman rule and a rise in Islamic piety led more and more North Africans to make the pilgrimage, or *hajj*, to Arabia. At the same time, the rise of European manufacturing slowly deepened North Africans' incorporation into transcontinental trade as producers of foodstuffs and luxury goods and as consumers of mass-produced items. At the same time, however, this integration could not entirely stave off several forces of destabilization that emerged midcentury. The first of these was the gradual decline of the central authority of the Ottoman sultans, which allowed their North African vassals in Tripoli, Algiers, and even Cairo to act with some autonomy. This was exacerbated by the second trend—the rise of Britain and France as Mediterranean players alongside North Africans, the Ottoman sultans, and the Portuguese, Spanish, and citizens of Italian kingdoms and city-states.

As a result, North Africa's rulers and elites were in the 1750s essentially independent players in the Mediterranean, under only loose Ottoman control. Although they frequently contributed to the sultan's treasury and called upon him in time of need, the authorities in Tunis and other urban centers often modified their policies to suit local needs and also independently made deals with Europeans and each other. As the eighteenth century came to a close, Ottoman authority declined even further, partly due to stirrings of rebellion in Arabia. The most significant of these uprisings was the orthodox Islamic movement known as Wahhabiyya, which was sponsored by the Saud family of the Arabian Peninsula and which rejected Ottoman tolerance for other religions and control over the holy city of Mecca. As a result, North Africa's leaders and societies were left with decisions to make about their political alignment, economics, and social situations.

In the far west of the African Mediterranean coastline, the state of Morocco was ruled by the descendants of Sultan Mawlay Isma'il, including, toward the end of the eighteenth century, the great king Muhammad III. Fully independent, Morocco was a society balanced between the cosmopolitanism of the urban, coastal cities and a reformist orthodoxy that was powerful in the rural areas. In the early nineteenth century, this balance turned to conflict when a new sultan, Mawlay Sulayman (1792–1822), began to embrace the orthodox Islamic conception of the state modeled on the Wahhabiyya in Arabia (see chapter 3). However, his reforms ran up against the opposition of the big trading families that dominated cities like Rabat, Tangier, and Fez. These mercantile elites resented the religious restrictions he placed on their ability to do business. The sultan might have been strong enough to overcome them if he had not at the same time picked a fight with the Berber communities of Morocco's interior. The Berbers largely practiced a form of Sufi Islam that Wahhabi leaders saw as heretical, and thus Mawlay Sulayman sought to force them to accept his orthodox religious practices. He combined this attack on their religious practices with an attempt to increase taxes and to normalize his authority over the Berbers, sending both an army and an enlarged bureaucracy to extend his control of the interior. The Berbers reacted through a military resistance that culminated in an 1819 battle in which they defeated Mawlay Sulayman, damaging his authority and reputation. His successors learned from his experience and chose to follow a more moderate path in both religious tolerance and tax policy, although they kept the enlarged bureaucracy he had built. The state these sultans ruled, by the mid–nineteenth century, was relatively strong—bound together by the sultan's alliances with leading commercial and religious families, a relatively strong and experienced standing army, and a cosmopolitan tolerance for religious differences. This strength would largely enable them to endure the challenge from Europeans in the mid–nineteenth century.

To the east of Morocco, however, the Tunisian beys faced deeper problems. They not only were beset by European challengers in the early nineteenth century but also encountered significant interference from Algeria's Ottoman governors, the deys of Algiers, who meddled in Tunisia's economy and periodically invaded the territory, ignoring the fact that both Tunisia and Algeria were technically provinces of the Ottoman Empire. In fact, the deys were already independently increasingly Algerian trade with Europeans, especially in the area of wheat exports. Although profitable for Algeria's rulers, however, this trade was unpopular among the Algerian people because it raised domestic food prices. The result was considerable unrest, especially during periods of bad rains. This unrest eventually led to rebellion and the assassination of seven deys in a row between 1807 and 1816. The resulting weakness of the state left the way open for a French invasion in 1827, the first step in France's long road to colonial rule in Algeria.

Between Algeria and Egypt, Libya was a battleground of diplomacy, piracy, and warfare for much of the eighteenth century. The key factions in this contest were alternately supported by the Ottoman sultans and by various European powers. In 1790, Ottoman loyalists regained the upper hand with the assistance of Tunisian ships and troops. However, to keep their troops happy, the new authorities had to allow significant numbers of them to operate as pirates preying on Mediterranean traffic from Libyan ports like Tripoli. These practices eventually led to war with the new United States of America, a war that Tripoli's rulers pursued with some success. In subsequent decades, however, they were not as successful in staving off British and French influence in the form of loans, which slowly increased the ability of European consuls to influence policy. Eventually, the pasha of Tripoli found himself caught between the demands of European bankers and consuls, on the one hand, and of his own merchant communities, on the other, leading to a civil war that was settled only by a further Ottoman intervention in 1835.

Egypt, meanwhile, was in the mid–eighteenth century more fully in the orbit of the Ottoman Empire than its neighbors to the west. The cultural ties between Ottoman society and Egypt led to the increasing cosmopolitanization of Cairo, an important imperial city protected by a significant Ottoman garrison. For example, both Turkish-language and Arabic literature, then popular in Istanbul and other major cities of the empire, spread to the literate classes of Cairo in this period. In the 1760s, political infighting led to a brief period of chaos that only ended with the rise of Ali Bey, a strongman backed by the Ottoman government who hoped he could end the chaos. Ali Bey's success, however, put him in a strong enough position to fashion himself as an autonomous ruler, coining his own money and setting his own economic policies. He also stimulated a sense of national identity among the urban classes of Egypt. The last decades of the eighteenth century were defined by attempts by the Ottomans to reassert themselves, broken largely by the invasion of Egypt by the French in 1798. Yet the French were unsuccessful in holding Egypt in the face of local forces supported by Britain, and their retreat in 1801 emboldened the Egyptian national movement. Partly as a result, when the Ottomans returned to power under a new viceroy—Muhammad Ali—the new administration chose to pursue a vision of an Egypt that was self-ruling, although still within the Ottoman Empire. To achieve this vision, Muhammad Ali played the great regional powers—the Ottoman sultans, Egypt, and France— against each other. He also initiated a series of reforms to strengthen and modernize the state, adapting many ideas and technologies from European states (see chapter 4).

The periodic flaring of conflict in all these provinces and countries during this period only marked their deepening integration into a transcontinental exchange across the Mediterranean Sea. Some of this trade was illicit—conducted through smuggling and piracy— although this decreased in the face of the consolidation of both European and North African state power after the 1780s. In this process, North Africa's leaders came to rely upon large mercantile concerns for tax revenues. The beys of Tunisia, for example, established close ties to both local Jewish commercial families and European corporations and often granted them monopolies in exchange for taxes. Similarly, in Algeria two local Jewish families controlled the grain trade in alliance with the state at least until 1805. In the following decades, however, European families came to dominate and finance an increasing number of commercial ventures in the area.

Commercial opportunities in North Africa attracted a number of Europeans and Turkic-speaking Ottoman citizens who settled in cities like Fez, Algiers, and Cairo during this time. They were followed by diplomats, or consuls. These diplomats at first just represented their governments to the authorities in Libya, Morocco, Tunisia, Algeria, and Egypt. Over time, however, they began to loan money to build up their own power structures, loaning money to rulers, supporting rebels, and generally changing the balance of society. In several big cities of the coast, they even negotiated to create independent zones where the local laws were not in effect. This was especially true in Algiers, but also in Tunis, which by the 1830s was involved in a tug-of-war between parties supporting France and those loyal to the Ottoman sultans. Even in Muhammad Ali's Egypt, European bankers allied with diplomats became increasingly influential in the 1840s.

In the early nineteenth century, Europeans' strategy of exerting diplomatic and economic power in the region was punctuated by a series of invasions of North Africa by France beginning with Napoleon's brief and unsuccessful invasion of Egypt in 1798. A more lasting episode began in 1827 with a French attack on Algiers. Yet this invasion was not immediately successful. Despite mobilizing overwhelming force, the invaders were in fact held at bay by two groups—an official resistance based in the eastern Algerian city of Constantine and a collection of rebels under the Sufi thinker and activist 'Abd al-Qadir in the west. Both groups were able to continue the fight against increasingly large French armies until 1847–1848, gaining support from neighboring states like Morocco and volunteers from around the region who filtered in through a network of the Qadiriyya Islamic brotherhoods (see chapter 3). Even after 1848, a series of uprisings kept the French unbalanced for decades.

'Abd al-Qadir's resistance attracted significant support because his vision of an egalitarian brotherhood of men tied together under Islamic law was immensely popular. He promoted this vision together with the types of reforms he had seen in Egypt and Arabia during his hajj to Mecca as a young man, and it attracted many followers. 'Abd al-Qadir was at one and the same time a man of the people and a smart, cosmopolitan diplomat who read French newspapers and negotiated with French military men and diplomats. He effectively established a government-in-resistance of the interior based partly on a bureaucratic system combining recognition of local chiefs and other notables with firm ties of Islamic brotherhood. At the same time, however, working through the Qadiriyya limited his ability to reach out to other Islamic brotherhoods, thus splitting his potential base. In 1843, he was driven into Morocco by a French expedition, where he found supporters and sympathizers. However, the Moroccan sultan Muhammad IV, fearful of French strength, treated 'Abd al-Qadir as an outlaw, and he was captured by a French force in 1847. Muhammad IV's collaboration with the French pursuit of 'Abd al-Qadir weakened his popularity in the country, but he gained back the people's support by carefully nurturing their national aspirations, especially during a Spanish invasion in 1859. His initial defiance of the Spanish stirred up his subjects' anger at both France and Spain and made the sultan the focus of Moroccan nationalism.

The French campaign in Algeria also brought a response from the Ottoman sultans, who in the 1830s forcefully reoccupied Tripoli to forestall an expansion of the French invasion to Libya. This was more than merely a military reoccupation, however, because the new arrivals brought with them the flourishing ideas and practices of Ottoman reformism (the *tanzimat*). The new administrators greatly strengthened Libyan civil society by encouraging urbanization, providing better security, creating new criminal courts staffed by professional judges, and helping to pay for newspapers, telegraphs, and a new postal system. They also allied with the local Sufi orders to provide more widespread education for both boys and girls.

By 1850, therefore, the Mediterranean frontier of Africa remained a cosmopolitan zone, under threat perhaps of European occupation but nevertheless a place where dynamic societies and their rulers strove to master the challenges of a shifting economic and political context.

ATLANTIC AFRICA

By contrast with trade in the African societies bordering the Mediterranean, intercontinental exchange on the Atlantic coast of Africa was a much newer trend. Both the vast distances of the Atlantic and the wind patterns off West Africa meant that extensive reciprocal trade and migration from Atlantic Africa dated back only to the fifteenth-century Spanish and Portuguese voyages of exploration. Yet from the moment that the first Portuguese ships rounded Cape Bojador and reached the mouth of the Senegal River, Africans had been active participants in the new intercontinental trading system connecting Europe, Africa, and the Americas.

Portuguese explorations had been incremental and initially aimed more at reaching Asia than at interacting with Africans. However, the Portuguese rapidly found African goods that they desired—gold, malagueta peppers, ivory, beeswax, and gum being chief among them. West and West-Central Africans were involved from the beginning not only as producers but also in the transportation and securing of goods across the oceans. Few were owners of the large oceangoing vessels that plied the Atlantic routes in this period, although some Africans owned large sailing vessels and canoes that were engaged in the local "coasting" trade. Additionally, Africans served in the tens of thousands as sailors; as soldiers in forts in Africa, Asia, and the Americas; and as interpreters, porters, and artisans across the Portuguese trading network.

However, the greatest force drawing Africans into the Atlantic world in the period leading up to and including the eighteenth century was the Atlantic slave trade, which by the 1850s had coerced approximately 11 to 12 million Africans into a forced migration to the Americas, Europe, and other parts of Africa. The Atlantic slave trade is heavily discussed in volume one of this series. However, any attempt to understand the Atlantic coast of Africa from 1750 to 1875 must include a survey of the trade's impact on the African continent. In fact, different parts of Atlantic Africa were affected in different ways and to various degrees, but several general conclusions can be made. First, large regions of Africa suffered significant demographic loss as productive members of society were enslaved and their communities torn apart in the slaving process. Even those inhabitants of these regions who evaded capture generally had to move to safer areas—swamps, mountains, forests, and caves—and thus lost much of their ability to produce food for themselves and as surplus. In addition, over time, many West and West-Central African societies underwent a social transformation as "big men"— those who could provide security through the use of force—came to replace more complex, egalitarian models of society suited to more peaceful times. These men took advantage of their position and power to increase their access not only to wealth and resources but also to women, causing polygamy to expand in many coastal societies. In some areas, these big men propped up growing states like Dahomey and Asante that profited from the Atlantic slave trade. In other areas their aspirations tore apart existing states. Both Kongo and the Jolof Confederation south of the Senegal River were dismembered in this way.

In the process, the Atlantic slave trade reoriented the web of economic ties in the area into a more directed coast-to-interior trading network, and European and American slave traders introduced new types of credit and debt arrangements to encourage local big men to cooperate with them. These new credit relationships helped to create the complex, cosmopolitan, but often hierarchical societies that emerged during the era of the Atlantic slave trade at the points of greatest interaction between Africans and Europeans—especially the towns clustered around major ports and trading positions on the Atlantic coast. These included islands like Saint-Louis on the Senegal River, castles built at the edges of existing towns like Elmina in the Gold Coast, and new urban centers like Freetown in Sierra Leone. These areas came to be the centers of creole societies—the term "creole" connoting the mixing of African, European, and in some cases Asian people, cultures, religions, and economies. Nor were creole societies just the sum of their parts. Rather, the cultural mixing set off a creative energy that gave birth to new, hybrid identities and processes of adaptation and invention.

The earliest Atlantic African creole societies were Afro-Portuguese, springing from early sixteenth-century Portuguese sailors and merchants who settled among local communities along the Guinea coast and Cape Verde. Their descendants identified themselves often as "Portuguese," by which they indicated several things: their involvement in commerce, at least some embrace of Catholicism (although many of their ancestors were actually Portuguese Jews), and their Portuguese-style architecture. They also considered themselves to be Portuguese-speakers, although for everyday use they developed a creole language that was partly based on Portuguese vocabulary but integrated local, African grammatical structures. By the late eighteenth century, with Portugal long in global decline, the self-described "Portuguese" of the African Atlantic coast were really members of a linked network of merchants and their families spread across western Africa, who often saw themselves as different both from Africans of the interior and from the newer groups of French, Dutch, and English merchants and administrators and their local mates and progeny. They continued to take Portuguese names even though many no longer practiced Catholicism or spoke even the Afro-Portuguese creole languages.

Among the non-Portuguese-speaking Atlantic creoles who emerged subsequently were the French-speaking *habitants* of West Africa of 1659. This community coalesced following the French seizure of Gorée Island in 1677 and Saint-Louis at the mouth of the Senegal River in 1659. They were a hybrid of French merchants trading in enslaved humans, gum, and other goods as well as administrators sent to run these small territories mixed with members of many African communities. Saint-Louis especially grew into a town whose free citizens included Afro-Portuguese and other African Catholics, Muslims including Maures from Mauritania and local Wolof-speakers as well as Fulbe-speakers from far upriver, and adventurers and craftspeople from other parts of Africa. The African citizens of these towns often married their daughters to French men, usually in ceremonies marked by both European and African rituals. By the late eighteenth century, *habitant* society was marked by many of the signs of the French-speaking world such as large houses with cast-iron balconies and great balls thrown by the women of the towns. In the 1820s, there was even an attempt to build Louisiana-style plantations up the Senegal River.

Another creole community developed at the other extreme of Africa's Atlantic coast, in Cape Town near the southern tip of Africa. Cape Town had been founded by officers and servants of the Dutch East India Company in 1652. By the late eighteenth century, the territory it encompassed included both the city itself and surrounding rural districts under its control. This was an intensely cosmopolitan society inhabited by Khoi-speaking and isiXhosa-speaking Africans; Europeans including Dutch-, French-, and English-speakers; and both Chinese and Southeast Asian (Javanese, Sumatrian, Ambionese, and others) slaves and workers. In many ways, the city was a "tavern of the seas," with high rates of mixing among people of various groups. Yet these interactions could not disguise its underlying institutions of inequality. The enslavement of both Asians and Africans (legal until 1838) and laws to enforce their subjugation meant that identity differences were increasingly enforced throughout most of this period. At the same time, local Africans and Asians were often closely quartered, especially in the town itself but also in the rural areas surrounding it. This led to the development of a creole identity—later and controversially termed "coloured"—that took in many Asian forced immigrants but also included numerous local Africans and even some who were brought to the colony from elsewhere. Within this mix, a new language developed based on Dutch but with African and Asian vocabulary and a simplified grammar to cope with the many different speakers. This language, which became modern Afrikaans, at first developed among the farming and working classes of Europeans, Southeast Asians, and Africans. It was just one link between these communities, which lived in very close association with each other. Few houses in Cape Town, for example, had separate slave quarters, and there was, in this period, no racial segregation. At the same time, however, a racial hierarchy clearly developed in this period that excluded those not of European descent from access to wealth and positions of power.

The development of racial hierarchies and the practices of enslavement in Cape Town society reflected the widespread oppression of Africans and peoples of African descent in the Atlantic world. Partly because of this, Africans played a leading role in the revolts against oppression that characterized the Atlantic world between 1750 and 1875. Many of these were small-scale uprisings whose stories are not frequently told, such as the 500 or more shipboard revolts by enslaved Africans en route to the Americas. Africans also sought to evade or fight their enslavers by fleeing to defensible or less penetrable environments, changing their cultivation habits, undertaking informal boycotts of Europeans, and giving misinformation to raiders. They also altered their housing construction, village architecture, field arrangement, cultivation methods, settlement size, religion and rituals, central political institutions, and diplomatic arrangements to defend themselves against enslavement.

Africans were also key players in perhaps the most incredible of the revolutions in the Atlantic world in this period—the Haitian Revolution that culminated in the greatest and arguably most successful slave uprising of all times. Saint Domingue (Haiti) was just one of dozens of sugar colonies in the Caribbean and the American mainland in which, collectively, millions of slaves worked to produce wealth for European merchants, aristocrats, companies, and states. It was the crown jewel of French colonies in the eighteenth century, with the largest slave population and highest sugar production of all the Caribbean islands, as well as producing half of the world's coffee exports. About 40,000 white Frenchmen and almost as many free people of color also populated the French half of the island. These individuals took various sides in the French Revolution, sending representatives to Paris in 1789 and alternately championing the cause of the monarchy or the Republicans. However, few of them anticipated the impact the Revolution would have on the half million slaves of the colony. On August 22, 1791, hundreds of enslaved Africans and descendants of Africans launched a coordinated attack on plantations near the town of Cap François. Their rebellion was well organized and spread rapidly as it evolved into a truly revolutionary movement aimed at overturning the slave system of the island. This movement was successfully organized by leaders like François-Dominique Toussaint Louverture, a manumitted former slave whose father appears to have been enslaved in Allada, West Africa, and brought to Haiti as a plantation worker. Over the next decade, revolutionary armies under Louverture and his generals battled not only French but also British forces into submission and liberated the French half of the island. Thereafter, it became a base of revolutionary activity and ideology, giving temporary refuge to Simón Bolívar, among others. The slave rebellion in Haiti was undoubtedly the most far-reaching of the Atlantic revolutions, ending slavery and replacing a slave-owning aristocracy with a leadership drawn largely from among the enslaved.

Interestingly, when forced to choose sides in the battle between Republicans and Royalists in the French Revolution, both the leaders and the rank and file of the formerly enslaved Haitians seem to have aligned themselves with the French Royalists even while they fought to overthrow French rule in Haiti altogether. Was this because many of their former owners chose to support the Republican cause, or was there another explanation? Historian John Thornton has one such explanation that ties in well to the story of Beatriz Kimpa Vita related in chapter 1. Thornton suggests that the Royalist sentiments of the enslaved were in fact a carryover from the pro-unification and Kongolese royalist sentiments of the Antonian movement. Thornton suggests that many enslaved Kongolese transported to Haiti, and especially those who had been among Beatriz Kimpa Vita's followers, understood a king as the guardian of the type of social agreement that had once maintained a high standard of living in Kongo. They brought their longing for that kind of stability to Haiti with them, and it led them not only to support the Royalists in France but also to choose a very centralized type of government for themselves following their successful revolution in Haiti.

Haiti was not the only Atlantic revolution led by Africans, although it was the most successful. A second example took place in 1808 in the countryside near Cape Town. South African historian Nigel Worden, who has worked at length on this subject, has pointed out that the leaders of the uprising were three African slaves from Cape Town who had met in the port city a number of Atlantic revolutionaries. These included two Irish soldiers who had apparently told them that there was no slavery in Europe, as well as other sailors and transients who told them about revolutions in France and rebellions in the Americas. These three young African men also had observed the changes brought to this southern region of Africa by the British, who defeated the Dutch rulers of Cape Town in 1806 and abolished the Atlantic slave trade in the following year. Yet they were disappointed that, despite criminalizing the slave trade, the British did nothing to emancipate the slaves already in the region. Thus these three slave leaders attempted to replicate the revolution in Saint Domingue themselves. In the end, however, the 1808 uprising failed. The combination of a united front of Dutch-speaking settlers and British military units shut the rebels down in a way that had not been possible in much of the Americas. Nevertheless, the way in which it happened and the goals of its leaders suggest a common connection to events on the other side of the Atlantic.

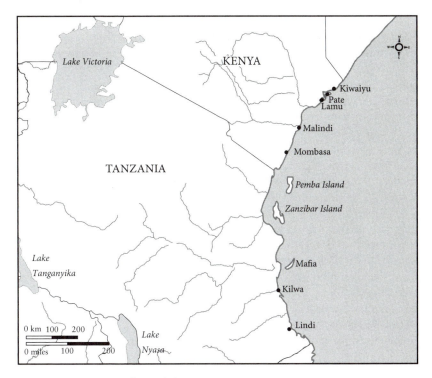

Lake Victoria

KENYA

Kiwaiyu
Pate
Lamu

Malindi

Mombasa

TANZANIA

Pemba Island

Zanzibar Island

Lake
Tanganyika

Mafia

Kilwa

Lindi

0 km 100   200

0 miles   100   200

Lake
Nyasa

MAP 3   Port cities of East Africa, c. 1840

INDIAN OCEAN AFRICA

Following the western coast of Africa, Portuguese adventurers and pirates in 1498 rounded the Cape of Good Hope and entered the Indian Ocean world. Unlike the societies of the Atlantic coast of Africa, however, those of the Indian Ocean edge of the continent had been engaged in intercontinental exchange and commerce for hundreds (and in some cases thousands) of years. The new European arrivals temporarily had a technological advantage over the locals in their ship-borne cannon and fast caravels, which they used to ransack the trading cities of the coast and waylay local merchant ships. They also managed to take over a portion of the shipping trade from East Africa to Arabia and India. However, their hegemony on the seas here was never complete. By the 1580s, the Portuguese caravels and galleons were heavily pressed by Ottoman, Iranian, and Omani (Arab) shippers.

The principal challenge to Portuguese control of East African trade before 1750, however, came from Swahili-speaking merchants who inhabited a broad swath of the coast from Mogadishu in the north to Mozambique in the south. Swahili-speaking society was highly cosmopolitan. Based largely on the Bantu-speaking population of East Africa, Swahili society had over the preceding millennium also integrated Somalis, Arabs, and South Asians. Swahili-speakers in turn left the continent to travel deep into the Indian Ocean as sailors and merchants, often setting up homes in Arabia and India. The key Swahili trading vessels were dhows, which evidence suggests were owned by collaborating groups of merchants who also owned parts of the cargo and who crewed the vessel as well. From about the eighth century onward, these dhows had helped knit together the people of the East African coast into a society with shared characteristics: a common language based on Bantu grammar but incorporating Arabic and Persian conventions and words, a key role in trade routes linking the African interior and Indian Ocean, a common religion in Islam, and a diverse but unified sense of aesthetics that included coral architecture and gold jewelry.

In the sixteenth and seventeenth centuries, these loose-knit Swahili-speaking communities were locked in intermittent conflict with Portuguese over who would control the large coastal trading towns and the trade that went through them. Seeking to drive out the Portuguese, the major Swahili sultanates in the seventeenth century sought alliances with Muslims from outside of Africa, including Omani aristocrats from the Arabian Peninsula. The Omani were already engaged in outright naval warfare against Portuguese in the Red Sea. Thus when the Swahili-speaking rulers of Mombasa and others turned to the sultan of Oman to help liberate them, he responded positively. Between 1698 and 1729, the sultan licensed Omani merchants to help fight the Portuguese and also brought his own royal vessels to the East African coast. As a result, the Portuguese were largely driven out of the region other than a few southern positions (now Mozambique). By the 1750s, however, the Omani merchant-sultan alliance found themselves in competition with another commercial "state," the English East India Company, which was licensed and supported by the kings of Great Britain. Taken together, these two groups made possible the increasing volume of trade and the large-scale movements of people that marked the next century in East African history.

To the Swahili-speakers, the Omani were potential allies against the Portuguese. For the Omani sultans, in turn, the lucrative Indian

Ocean trade in dates, ivory, spices, and other goods provided the funds they needed to pay for their conflict with religious dissidents. In this fight, Africans were useful to the sultans not only for the revenue they provided but also as both slave laborers and royal soldiers. Together, the Omani and their Swahili-speaking allies came in the eighteenth century to control much of the long-distance trade between East Africa and India, which was immensely lucrative. They then solidified this position by turning their British competitors into allies through a series of negotiations and treaties. Even together, however, they never had a complete monopoly on local trade, and in many cases their worst competitors were rival Omani princes and dissident Swahili merchants who competed to control trade to and from different East African cities. It was in order to get a grip on this problem that Sultan Seyyid Said moved his royal court to Zanzibar in East Africa in 1838.

Both the Omani sultans and those Swahili city-states that remained independent in this period were tightly tied not only into the Indian Ocean trade but also into commerce with African peoples in the interior. In the eighteenth century, especially, new trade routes were constructed from their coast cities deep into the interior. In the south, towns like Kilwa were linked with peoples of the interior like the Nyamwezi and Yao who hunted for ivory and helped to transport

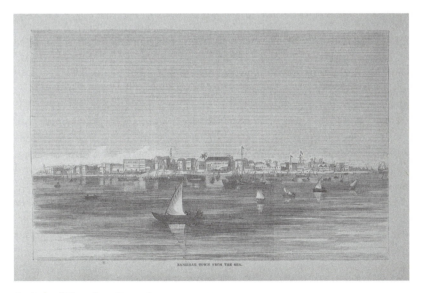

A view of Zanzibar from the sea, c. 1850

gold. By the nineteenth century, these trade routes had grown to such importance that large communities of Swahili-speakers began moving from the coastal towns to the interior to organize caravans and buy goods more cheaply.

By this time, Swahili society was more cosmopolitan than ever, taking in the practices and ideas of new communities within Africa, as well as Omani and other migrants from Asia. In the interior of what is today Tanzania, urban zones formed around groups of traders from the coast who intermarried with local women in the early nineteenth century. By the 1850s, Swahili-speaking traders had penetrated deep into the Great Lakes kingdoms of Buganda and possibly Bunyoro. It even seems possible that they reached Luanda, on the opposite coast of Africa, although they did not set up a permanent community there. Meanwhile, Omanis and many Indians working for the Omani court became integrated into the coastal Swahili communities. In addition, towns like Zanzibar became home to even more distant trading and diplomatic communities, with embassies from Britain, the United States, Germany, and other states.

According to historian Randall Pouwels, this transformation had an effect on the social organization of the older Swahili city-states. The arrival of Omani and Arab rulers and the establishment of royal courts, for example, may have changed notions of what it meant to be "civilized" among Swahili-speakers. In the eighteenth century, the dominant idea of a civilized person within Swahili society, Pouwels argues, "centered on the ideal of the free, cultured, indigenous townsperson who was thoroughly schooled in local language, tradition, and forms of Islam." (p. 413) By the early nineteenth century, however, an upper class had emerged that largely adopted Arab lifestyles, literacy in both Arabic and Swahili, and Arab forms of Islamic worship as symbols of civilization. This group increasingly distanced itself from lower classes of Swahili townspeople. They came to embrace an "Indian Ocean" identity very strongly, although not necessarily a racialized one. Instead, wealth and the adoption of Arabic and Persian cultural activities and possessions marked out status in this society Some scholars have suggested that this was reflected even in architecture, as two-level houses became the norm in big towns like Lamu, with upper classes occupying the upper floors and renting out the lower floors to families and individuals whom they saw as lower class.

The Omani commercial state based in Zanzibar was the leading but not the only international network linking East Africa with the Indian Ocean. Other systems existed outside of its orbit, including the shrunken

Portuguese system that controlled small enclaves on the coast of what is today Mozambique and up the Zambezi River, as well as a French system that took in the Indian Ocean islands of Mauritius and the Masacrenes with some influence upon states and societies on the island of Madagascar. Yet the ports and trading entrepôts of these regions also developed a sort of cosmopolitanism that spanned identities and continents. These will be discussed further in chapters 3 and 4.

The Chronicles of Pate and Nineteenth-Century Swahili Identity

Like heterogeneous societies the world over, the Swahili-speaking communities of eighteenth- and nineteenth-century East Africa found ways to bind their cosmopolitan population together partly by creating stories, myths, and histories that presented a shared past. A number of these stories took the shape of chronicles that purported to tell the story of the founding of the community and its subsequent history. In some cases, these histories or stories actually dated back to that founding, but in most cases they were developed much later.

The chronicles of the history of the Swahili-speaking town of Pate are a case in point. Pate was a leading Swahili polity in the sixteenth and seventeenth centuries, although its importance declined in later centuries. Eventually, the city was occupied by the British, who sacked the royal palace of the sultans of Pate in 1895. In the process, they destroyed the written chronicles, and thus left us only with orally related versions. Historian Marina Tolmacheva collected eight versions of this chronicle, all of which are attributed to Muhammad bin Fumo 'Umar Nabahani, also known as Bwana Kitini. Bwana Kitini was a member of Pate's ruling family in the nineteenth century, and he passed on the oral versions of the chronicles to members of his family or related them to Europeans who wrote them down.

The chronicles as told by Bwana Kitini discuss the founding of Pate in the early thirteenth century, but they appear to tell us more about the ways that eighteenth- and nineteenth-century inhabitants of Pate created a vision of a shared past than about the founding itself. The accounts focus on the supposed arrival of an Arab noble—Seleman, of the Nabahani family—and his marriage to the daughter of the African king of Pate. One version narrated by Kitini tells the story this way:

> The first man who came (to Pate), among the Nabhans, was Seleman son of Seleman, son of Muthafar the Nabhan, with his brothers, Ali bin Seleman and Athman bin Seleman. He who was the Sultan was this Seleman aforesaid, and he was king

in Arabia and was driven out by the Ya'arubi and came to Pate in the year 600 (six hundred) of the Hijra [1203–1204 CE]. … He married the daughter of the King of Pate, Batawîna. And the custom of the Swahili, to this day, is this: if a man marries your daughter, when the seven days of the wedding are finished, he goes to see his wife's father, (who) gives him something—this is the usage of all the Swahili. When Seleman went to see him, (his father-in-law) handed over the kingdom to him. From thenceforth he reigned, the aforesaid Seleman bin Seleman. (Werner 1915, p. 513)

How should we understand this story? Bwana Kitini himself was a member of the Nabahani royal family of Pate, and it is probable that the versions of the Pate chronicle he related were meant to legitimize his family's rule of the area prior to the British conquest. The Nabahani claim that their ancestors ruled Pate as far back as the thirteenth century, although this is probably not accurate. Other evidence, from sources not directly involved in local political struggles, suggests the Nabahani actually only became rulers of this area in the late seventeenth or early eighteenth century. Therefore, it is possible that this story was largely invented to legitimize their rule. At the same time, however, it is too much to suggest that these accounts represent *only* the claims to historical legitimacy of the ruling family. We know from other sections of the account that in the nineteenth century groups of African commoners ("the people") were able to replace unpopular Afro-Omani rulers of Pate if they felt that they had lost the right to rule. Thus the chronicles probably also represent an attempt to acknowledge the connection between the African roots of much of the population and the Omani roots of the Nabahani family. This unity, represented by the marriage narrative, was meant to cement both civil order and the rule of the royal family as representatives of this union. Thus from this source, we can know something about how Swahili-speakers of Pate sought to cope with and master the challenges and opportunities of living as inhabitants of Africa in an oceanic age.

REFERENCES

Mediterranean Africa

Abun-Nasr, Jamil. *A History of the Maghrib in the Islamic Period* (Cambridge: Cambridge University Press, 1987).

Clancy-Smith, Julia. *Rebel and Saint: Muslim Notables, Populist Protest, Colonial Encounters, Algeria and Tunisia, 1800–1904* (Berkeley: University of California Press, 1994).

Atlantic Africa
Thornton, John. *Africa and Africans in the Making of the Atlantic World, 1400–1800* (Cambridge: Cambridge University Press, 1992).

Worden, Nigel, Elizabeth van Heyningen, and Vivian Bickford-Smith. *Cape Town: The Making of a City*, (Cape Town: New Africa Books, 2011).

Indian Ocean Africa
Gilbert, Erik. "Coastal East Africa and the Western Indian Ocean Region: Long-Distance Trade, Empire, Migration, and Regional Unity, 1750–1970." *History Teacher* 36 (2002): 7–34.

Pouwels, Randall L. "Eastern Africa and the Indian Ocean to 1800: Reviewing Relations in Historical Perspective." *International Journal of Historical Studies* 35 (2002): 413.

Sheriff, Abdul. *The Dhow Culture of the Indian Ocean: Cosmopolitanism, Commerce and Islam* (New York: Columbia University Press, 2010).

The Chronicles of Pate and Nineteenth-Century Swahili Identity
Pouwels, Randall L. "The Pate Chronicles Revisited: Nineteenth-Century History and Historiography." *History in Africa* 23 (1996): 301–318.

Tolmacheva, Marina. *The Pate Chronicles* (East Lansing: Michigan State University Press, 1993).

Werner, Alice, "A Swahili History of Pate." *Journal of the Royal African Society* 14 (1915): 153.

3

Spiritual Belief and Practice in Cosmopolitan Africa

AFRICAN "WORLD" AND AFRICAN "TRADITIONAL" RELIGIONS

Just as generations of Western scholars studying social structures in the eighteenth and nineteenth centuries create a false dichotomy between African "tribes" and Eurasian "nations," so too writers on Africans' spiritual past have often divided the "world" religions of Islam, Christianity, and (more rarely) Judaism from African "traditional" religions. This idea of a strict division between the globe-spanning organized religions and more localized African faiths would have been unrecognizable to Africans of this period. Rather, as increasing numbers of Africans encountered Islam and Christianity, they tended to fit them alongside or within their spiritual worldviews instead of seeing them as something very different from their own sets of beliefs and practices. In fact, both for these widespread religions and for local faiths, the word "religion" is somewhat misleading. Instead, the evidence suggests that Africans in this era tended to see spirituality as deeply integrated into their social and cultural lives rather than separable from them. Africans had many names for the spiritual conceptions, practices, and ceremonies that fit in integrated

46

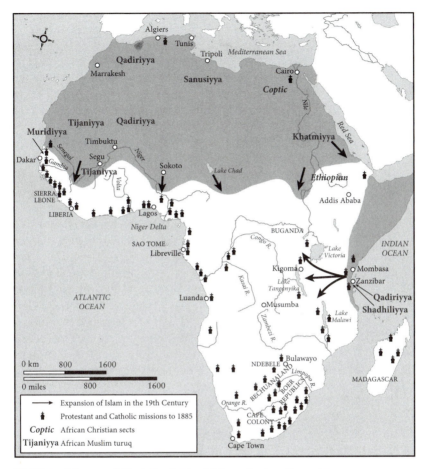

MAP 4   Islam and Christianity in Africa, nineteenth century

ways into their everyday lives as well as major rituals of personal, communal, and national strife, crisis, and celebration.

Moreover, African spiritual practice between approximately 1700 and 1875 was as cosmopolitan as African politics, commerce, and demographics. In many regions, there was no single "traditional religion" but rather a multifaceted, flexible, and often quite open set of practices and faiths that changed rapidly and accepted new ideas and practices imported from outside or invented by internal innovators.

When Islam and Christianity found their ways into these cosmopolitan settings, it was often through local individuals who reworked them to be usable by society. Admittedly, in the early nineteenth century Africans encountered two religious sects that were much more orthodox and less adaptable—evangelical Protestantism and Wahhabi Islam. To some degree, this chapter is about the strategies Africans adopted in dealing with these sects. However, African societies also continued to change and adapt even these faiths to their own needs.

The stories of Wahhabiyya and Protestantism in eighteenth- and nineteenth-century Africa are woven throughout this chapter but cannot be told until we have some understanding of the scope and facets of religion and spirituality in African societies around 1700. In describing this spiritual engagement we can begin with cosmology, a worldview or way of understanding the human relationship to the natural and supernatural worlds. Such cosmologies often include ancestors, gods and other types of deities, nature spirits, and creatures that cross between these worlds. The type of Sufi Islam that was practiced in much of western, northern, and coastal East Africa around 1700, for example, embraced the idea of human "mystic and intuitive experience" allowing for interaction with the will of Allah and the organization of the universe. Such cosmologies were related to the sense of moral and ethical values that defined communities. The dominant cosmology among the Dogon people of the West African Sahel, for example, venerated an orderly plan of the universe that was disrupted by an evil figure, Yurugu (the pale fox), who represented the negative value of chaos. Thus it upheld order as a beneficial value and chaos as something to be avoided. This is similar to the Kongolese promotion of balance and rejection of greed discussed in chapter 1.

Most often, eighteenth-century African cosmologies included some concept of the supernatural. With surprising frequency, this included the sense of a single supreme being, although often supported by many additional deities (gods and demigods). Local variations on the conception of the supreme being can be determined somewhat from the names given to them. The linguistic roots of some African names for a supreme being include "to mold," "to organize," "to give birth," and "to sprout" but also "the greatest," "the "all-knowing," and "the merciful." Others relate to a sense of coming from the sky, bringing rain, or performing particular useful tasks. Often, this paramount god was assisted by subordinate spirits and deities and ancestors, many of which were borrowed from neighboring societies. Igbo-speaking communities of this period were especially localized and diverse in their pantheons, which included unique collections of ancestors, spirits, and gods. In Asante, by contrast, there was a greater consensus on the makeup of the spiritual hierarchy, which included a supreme god (Nyame), multiple personal deities (*abosom*), ancestral figures (*samanfo*), and magical charms through which the ancestors and deities could be invoked (*suman*).

Many African societies of this period also had conceptions of negative agents that we today have come to label "witches" or "sorcerers," although these terms are often misleading because they developed in a European context. These agents could be supernatural, although Africans in this period often portrayed them as manifested in human form. There is evidence from Central and southern societies in this period that many communities saw the negative powers employed by these agents to be the cause of both individual and societal misfortunes—everything from illness to civil wars. On the other hand, however, some humans could act as "healers," using their faith and religious practices to "cure" both illness and social disorder. Thus many Africans whom we label priests or witch doctors were involved in psychological, political, and social healing practices, and their "medicine" was meant to facilitate those practices. Such medicine included not only substances and rituals but also powerful shrines, all of which were meant to help overcome conflict and social disorder. In some cases, political figures such as the Buganda king, or *kabaka*, were seen as being especially potent and had many medicinal rituals surrounding them that helped to unify society. Of course, this meant that religious practice was also a place of political contest, with different groups competing to own medicines such as religious rituals or holy sites.

Religious rituals were then, as now, important both to individual development and to civic society. Diviners used rituals to determine the sources of problems, and priests to heal societies. Rituals of passage marked birth, coming-of-age, elevations in rank and status, and death. Others marked the days of the calendar, the cycle of the years, and major social and political changes like the enthroning of rulers. Of course, because religion was inextricably connected to politics, law, and social structure, much of this chapter is devoted to these themes as well.

While many of these practices, cosmologies, and religious organizations were relatively localized in Africa, others reached across large regions and even outside the continent. In the eighteenth century, these included Judaism, Islam, and Christianity. Judaism had its origins just outside of Africa, and Jews have a long history in northern Africa and the Horn. By 1750, significant Jewish communities still existed in Egypt,

Morocco, and Ethiopia, and smaller communities occurred among Portu-guese-speakers in West Africa, although they were fading in other regions of North Africa. Islam had arrived on the continent in the era of the life of the prophet Muhammad, spreading across Egypt and the Maghreb from the seventh century c.e. and also appearing not long after in East African as a trading religion (c. 780). It remained a minor faith in that region until the thirteenth century, when Kiswahili-speakers adopted it and began to make it their own. Similarly, it crossed the Sahara into the West African Sahel also as a trading religion around the eleventh century but only really began to filter into wide sections of society as West Africans shaped it to fit into their cosmologies and social structures. Christianity, too, is an old religion in Africa. The largest significant population of Christians in the third century c.e. could be found in Egypt, where the intellectual envi-ronment of Alexandria proved a fertile ground for the Christian Gnostics, while the open desert of the Egyptian interior was the birthplace of the Christian monastery. By the seventh century various forms of Christian-ity existed across North Africa, with particular African sects centered upon Egypt and Nubia (Coptic), Ethiopia (Abyssinian), and among the Berbers and Tuareg of the Maghreb and Sahara (Donatism). Some of these sects faded with the arrival of Islam in North Africa, although the Coptic and Abyssinian churches continued to thrive. In the fifteenth cen-tury, Catholicism was brought to West Africa by Portuguese and Italian monks and priests. Here, and especially in Kongo and Benin, it quickly became Africanized as well. Thus we can say that both Islam and Chris-tianity were present in Africa in the 1700s through a variety of localized practices, many of which were mixed (or syncretized) with cosmologies and practices adapted from other African religions.

AFRICAN ISLAM IN THE EIGHTEENTH CENTURY

In the eighteenth century, most African Muslims subscribed to one of the many Sufi *turuq* (singular: *tariqa*). Each *tariqa* was a group of peo-ple built around a set of intellectuals, a system of rites and practices, and a particular way of understanding the word of the supreme being Allah and the ordering of the universe. Such *turuq* had thrived for hundreds of years in North Africa. In the cosmopolitan period of the eighteenth century, however, the place of the *turuq* in society began to shift as male brotherhoods within them became more coherent and centralized, evolving hierarchies that included ranks and rites of passage meant to propel the adherent upward. Across Islamic Africa, these *turuq* became political players, perhaps partly in response to the weakening of preexisting African political institutions due to the slave trade, or conversely as a result of their role in the growing commercial opportunities stretching across and beyond the continent.

Perhaps the most significant of the *turuq* in North and West Africa in this period was the Tijaniyya *tariqa*. Tijaniyya expanded rapidly in the late eighteenth century under the guidance of the disciples of Ahmad al-Tijani (1737–1815) of Algeria, for whom it was named. Al-Tijani taught that the universe is lit by the divine luminance of the "Light of Muhammad," underlying a celestial architecture that ordered the universe. Individual members of the *tariqa* aspired to interpret this celestial architecture, something that was only possible through individual meditation that took the form of communion with the prophet Muhammad. Marking this process, they could rise through several layers of "initiation" similar to those that that Al-Tijani believed the Prophet himself went through. These layers formed a hierarchy from carnal nature through heart, intellect, immortal spirit, and finally the knowledge of the divine secrets. The practice of Tijaniyya faith also had certain rituals and key beliefs. For example, practitioners could invoke the blessings of the Prophet and key holy men and undergo the ritual of visiting the graves of these holy men who could also perform miracles. Among the symbols and tools of members were Koranic amulets, the rosary, and occult letters and numbers drawn from the Koran. Practitioners were also enjoined to give alms for the memory of the dead and to remove their shoes in the presence of holy men.

As a package, Tijaniyya spread rapidly in North Africa both during and after the life of Al-Tijani. However, it quickly ran into opposition from more orthodox schools of Islamic thought spreading from the Arabian Peninsula. The greatest of these was Wahhabiyya (Wahhabism), which sought to purge the faith of "impurities" such as those of the North African *turuq* and return it to strict study of the Koran as a set of laws for virtuous living. Wahhabism was championed in North Africa by the Moroccan sultan Mawlay Sulayman (see chapter 2).

Tijaniyya and Wahhabiyya both moved into West Africa at approximately the same time. Islam was, of course, already in practice in the Sahelian zone of West Africa in 1700, although it was mainly the religion of rulers and a small literate elite, merchants who interacted with North African Muslims, and a number of pastoral communities. Most peasant cultivators in the Sahel and most forest dwellers were relatively unexposed to the religion. This changed, however, with the adoption of both orthodox and Tijaniyya ideals by inhabitants of the region in this period.

The context of this adoption was the Atlantic slave trade (see volume 1) and the failure of many of the existing states of Senegambia and the Niger River Bend to ably defend their populations from the predations of slavers. Indeed, along the Senegal River and elsewhere the military elites of many states turned to slave raiding themselves. The victims of these predations were typically peasants and herders, who eventually sought a means to unify so as to defend themselves against enslavement and in many cases against their own states. One alternative was provided by local Muslim intellectuals who journeyed to North Africa or even Mecca and returned with the support and legitimacy to build Islamic anti–slave trade movements. Their worldviews were rapidly adopted by pastoralists such as the Fulani and Tukolor of the Sahel and more slowly by cultivators in Senegambia and the Niger River area.

Probably the most successful of these warrior-intellectuals was Shehu Usuman dan Fodio. Dan Fodio emerged from a late eighteenth-century context of Hausa-dominated states in which Islamic reformers were already beginning to preach and to create autonomous Muslim communities, especially among the minority Fulani-speaking pastoralists who lived in these states. Around 1788, the Hausa-speaking kings of the region began to try to suppress the reformers, partly by persecuting the Fulani-speakers as a group. Dan Fodio, who had been taught by North African Islamic intellectuals, led his community of Fulani-speaking Muslims into rebellion against the ruler of Gobir, the state in which he lived, in 1804. Their initial success encouraged them to attack neighboring Hausa-speaking rulers. Eventually, their victories culminated in the building of a vast state that became known as the Sokoto Caliphate. Dan Fodio largely practiced an orthodox interpretation of Islam similar to that of Wahhabiyya and sought to strip away "extraneous" innovations and impose a stricter administration of Shari'a as well as observance of *ihsan* (good conduct). He used these concepts to organize a rational state structure based partly on that of the earlier, Baghdad-centered Abbasid Caliphate. As a federalized theocracy, the Sokoto administration gave a great deal of power to local governors, or emirs, who were trained as Islamic judges and who promoted a strict version of Shari'a. Dan Fodio also promoted a number of Islamic schools and built mosques around the region.

Other Islamic revolts against existing state structures that began in West Africa in this period were inspired by less orthodox versions of

Islam, and especially Tijaniyya. El Hajj Umar al-Futi (Umar Tal), for example, led a revolution among both Fulani-speaking cultivators and neighboring Wolof-speakers and Maures around the Senegal River in the 1840s. Al-Futi had both traveled through North Africa and Arabia and lived in Sokoto before returning to his home near the Senegal River, where his preaching attracted support from local peasants, many of whom lived in communities victimized by the slave trade and also threatened by French incursions. While in North Africa, Al-Futi had been charged by Tijani leaders with promoting Islam in West Africa, and he united the communities of the upper Senegal River through the promotion of the Tijaniyya brotherhood and values and the use of members of the tariq as military leaders. The state he created—the Umarian Empire—was run largely by a network of brotherhood members, and it expanded rapidly before his death. He is thus remembered largely as a political leader, although he was also a scholar of great repute, writing about faith and Islamic legal matters. Both within his domains and in surrounding areas, the Tijaniyya gained enormous strength during this period as a sect of the people.

Yet while we can talk of the Sokoto Caliphate and the Umarian state as related Islamic uprisings, it is important to note that orthodox and Sufi forms of Islam did not always act in concert. Al-Futi, for example, dedicated much of his life to overthrowing "pagan" societies but in the end was opposed by the more orthodox Muslim rulers of the Niger River state of Masina. They in turn were willing to ally themselves with non-Muslim Bamana regimes to oppose the Umarian state and justified the alliance partly by calling Tijani practices heretical. Ironically, one ruler of Masina, Seku Amadu Bari, himself came under fire for what some Muslim leaders in the region considered loose attention to Islamic law. Others, like the attempted revolutionary al-Hajj Mahmud, were considered too orthodox by Muslim merchants who wished to have a freer hand in trading goods and making money without the interference of strict Islamic laws and ethics.

In East Africa, meanwhile, Islam was expanding into the interior in the eighteenth century and early nineteenth century. At the northern end of the region, pastoralists such as Galla-speakers introduced Islamic practice and cosmology to the area west and north of Ethiopia, supported in the nineteenth century by the Egyptian conquerors of the Sudan. To the south, the spread of Islam was jump-started by the victory of the Omani Busaidi family over the Portuguese and their local allies and their development of a trading empire based on Zanzibar (see chapter 2).

This political transformation wrought by the creation of the Busaidi state of Zanzibar brought a series of interlinked political and religious changes to the region that promoted the spread of Islam. First, the relocation of the Busaidi helped to create a group of Islamic merchants and plantation owners within Swahili society, many of whom soon developed commercial ties to the societies of the interior. This class showed their wealth and displayed their power by building mosques and schools as well as extending their patronage to clerical individuals and groups in and around Zanzibar. They also created a large class of enslaved workers, who may also have adopted Islam, since they were allowed by law to convert and since Muslims may have enjoyed some additional protections under the law. Although this conversion may not have allowed the enslaved to rise rapidly in the class structure of Zanzibar and its tributary cities, evidence suggests that many of the captives *were* at least taught the Koran, and some may have adopted the faith completely.

Second, as the Muslim merchant and landowning class began to buy land in the East African interior, they brought Islam with them. In some cases, local people in these areas seem to have voluntarily adopted Islam, partly through intermarriage with Kiswahili-speaking Muslims. This appears to have been the case among the Segeju by 1854 and Digo-speakers in the 1860s. The type of Islam they practiced seems to have been relatively orthodox, although the Islamic law that came with it incorporated many local institutions, especially matrilineality in terms of inheritance. By the mid–nineteenth century, meanwhile, small Muslim enclaves were developing around caravan stops and trading posts even deep in the Central African interior. At this time, however, there is little evidence of widespread conversion in Central Africa, and many locals, including the Nyamwezi leader Mirambo, were hostile to Islam and forcibly opposed its spread.

Islam also spread in nineteenth-century southern Africa. Muslim communities had existed at the Dutch colony at the Cape of Good Hope as early as the seventeenth century. Many of the faith's first practitioners in this area were Malay and Indonesian political prisoners and captives of the Dutch East India Company. Perhaps partly because they came from many different parts of Southeast Asia, these communities elected a host of religious leaders and followed numerous religious and worship styles, some of which were quite orthodox, but others incorporating spirit and ancestor veneration or personal meditation practices. The Dutch rulers of the colony generally allowed Muslims to practice their faith, although they banned some mystical practices, particularly those of the Shafi'a sect. By the 1750s, a stream of African inhabitants of the colony, especially the enslaved, were converting to Islam. This may have been partly because enslaved Africans were not allowed to convert to the Protestant faith of the Dutch (Dutch Reformed Church) but as Muslims could partake in a number of the political and legal rights enjoyed by Christians and extended by law to Muslims, but not to Africans of other faiths. Following the British acquisition of the colony in the early nineteenth century, a number of Africans liberated from slave-trading vessels by the British navy were landed at the colony and also converted to Islam. The Muslim population of the region was also invigorated by a new group of Muslim immigrants who arrived in the 1860s—indentured Indians brought to work in the sugarcane fields and farms of Natal.

As in other parts of Africa, Islam in southern Africa in the nineteenth century experienced several attempts to rein in the freewheeling diversity of sects and practices and to introduce a more orthodox and strict Muslim community. In the Cape Colony and Natal, this effort was especially stimulated by Muslim clerics—in this case the Kurdish religious thinker Shaykh Abu Bakr Effendi—and supported by the British governors. However, it largely failed to discipline the cosmopolitan religious style of Cape Town's and Natal's Muslim communities, who continued to employ a wide variety of practices and to follow a great diversity of styles of worship.

AFRICAN CHRISTIANITY AND PROTESTANT EVANGELISM

Just as orthodox Muslim and Sufi intellectuals and teachers championed new styles of Islamic worship, ethical cosmologies, and religious practices to new parts of Africa in the eighteenth and nineteenth centuries, so too European and African missionaries advocated a new type of evangelical Christianity in the continent during this period. Their advocacy was based on a missionary ethic that had emerged strongly in Europe in the eighteenth century. The new ethic was in turn connected to the rise of a middle class of merchants and professionals who embraced the Christian ideals of the Protestant Reformation. Among the most important of these values for those denominations that led the missionary movement were the free will of the individual in choosing to believe in God, prayer in the language of the believer rather than Latin, the celebration of faith in Jesus Christ as the only way to achieve personal salvation, and a rejection of the authority of the pope and the Catholic Church. Many of these Protestant faiths— Wesleyan Methodists, Baptists, Quakers, and others—felt called to evangelize, that is, to testify to and share their faith and ideals with others. This calling for members to spread "the good word" connected individuals in a shared sense of responsibility and stimulated the establishment of an organizational logistics to support the mission of evangelizing others.

At first, these missionary logistics were purely domestic, as middle-class Protestants went out to preach to the working classes and poor in their own homes—especially Britain, Germany, Belgium, Switzerland, and the United States. In the 1780s, however, evangelical churches became involved in spreading their faith more widely, including in Africa. This turning outward reflected an awareness of Africa, Asia, and the Americas as fields with great potential for conversion. In looking at Africa, European evangelism was combined with abolitionism. The evangelical Protestant faiths in the 1790s through 1830s were at the center of the antislavery movement because of their belief in free will, their connections to middle-class groups in Europe and the United States whose domestic political opponents were slave-owning aristocrats, and their anticipation of evangelizing ex-slaves. It was this combination that led to the growth of movements that began to send missionaries to Africa in the early nineteenth century. By the 1850s, these included a large number based in Britain such as the London Missionary Society, the Congregational Missionary Society, the Wesleyan Methodist Missionary Society, and the Baptist Missionary Society. Others, such as the Rhenish Missionary Society and Basel Missionary Society, came out of Switzerland and Germany. They were joined by a few North Americans and later by French Catholics such as the White Fathers and the Sisters of Saint Joseph of Cluny, who were mostly based on Gorée Island off the coast of Senegal. These missionaries largely located themselves at the points of European influence all over Africa, although only a very few were in Muslim North Africa in this period.

The story of Protestant missionism in Africa from 1750 to 1875 necessarily begins in Europe. In telling it, however, the emphasis rapidly moves to Africa for at least three reasons. First, the most successful missionaries were Africans. Women such as Bribrina in the Niger delta spread Christianity widely among communities into which they married. Other leading missionaries were Africans of the diaspora. Catholicism, for example, only began to spread widely in West Africa when Brazilian Catholics reached Benin in the nineteenth century. Similarly, one of the leading early supporters of Christianity in Sierra Leone was Paul Cuffee, a former slave in the United States and a Quaker, who financed part of the settlement.

Second, these early African and diasporic missionaries rapidly adapted evangelical Christianity to focus on messages that reflected their own interpretations of Christianity. Specifically, they drew deeply on the story of bondage and freedom in the book of Exodus and elevated the place of Egypt and Ethiopia in the biblical narratives and the psalms, focusing especially on Psalm 68, which states, "Princes shall come out of Egypt, Ethiopia shall stretch forth her hands unto god." These ideas would eventually lead to the development of "Zionist" and "Ethiopian" African churches that focused on the notion of a place of salvation (Zion) and of the message of self-rule and independence (Ethiopia). That is a story that belongs properly in the colonial era, however.

Third, African reactions to the missionaries quickly became of key importance to the story of evangelical Protestantism in the continent. Local leaders reacted in a variety of ways to the arrival of missionaries. Some, like the *kabaka* (king) of Buganda, sought to use them for their own needs. Others, like Lobengula of the Shona or (in West Africa) the rulers of Asante and Dahomey refused to allow missions to be established, seeing them as a threat to society. Those rulers who did convert, like Agonglo of Dahomey in 1797, were sometimes replaced by their own people. In other cases, local leaders sought to moderate/mediate conversion. For example, the king of Onitsha in 1868 allowed his followers to attend church but sought to regulate religious intermarriage and Christian rituals.

Relations between missionaries and local leaders were frequently quite complex. An example of this can be found among the BaTswana in southern Africa. When members of the London Missionary Society arrived among the BaTswana in the 1820s, local leaders largely accepted them but asked in return for material gifts. Once the missionaries were allowed to set up a station, they won some converts but only by preaching among the politically powerless. By the mid-1830s, however, they felt strong enough to challenge local religious rituals, especially the rites of rainmaking. Some of the BaTswana leaders largely saw this as an attack on their political power, which was deeply interwoven with the rituals, and began to restrict the power of the missionaries and their converts. Yet when European settlers and treasure seekers began to impinge upon BaTswana land in the 1840s, coming north out of the Cape Colony, the BaTswana chiefs and elders responded by recruiting the missionaries as potential allies, and the two groups reached an accommodation that culminated in several missionaries supplying firearms to the BaTswana.

During this period, the attitudes of the bulk of the BaTswana toward Christianity also shifted. At first, most members of the local society had been put off by the exclusivism of Christianity, which demanded that they abandon all their other gods, cosmologies, and ways of worship. This exclusivism was as pronounced in evangelical Protestantism as it was for orthodox Muslims, marking the two as different from Sufi Islam, which tended to be more accepting of the cosmopolitan nature of most African religious communities. Those BaTswana who chose to convert had to make a major shift in their belief structure and lifestyles, and therefore among the BaTswana and many other African communities the first converts to Protestantism were mainly poor and politically powerless people seeking a new sense of community and support structure. Over time, however, the opportunities offered by Christianity became more attractive while, at least before the 1880s, the missionaries came to be somewhat more accepting of the diverse attitudes and approaches of locals who professed the faith.

The center of evangelical Protestantism in Africa was undoubtedly the colony of Sierra Leone, begun in 1787 when British abolitionists settled 411 black Europeans at a small settlement that they called Freetown. In 1791, at the instigation of a freed slave named Thomas Peters, the British government began to investigate resettling black loyalists who had supported Britain in the American Revolutionary War. Eventually, 1,190 of these loyalists would be resettled in Freetown. They were soon joined by captured maroons from Jamaica—enslaved Africans who had rebelled against the British rulers of that island. Many of these groups were already baptized Christians, either members of established evangelical Protestant churches or originators of their own Christian sects. Their presence attracted the Church Missionary Society, which became involved in the early 1800s and at least verbally supported local self-governance and the development of a Christian, democratic society.

The new settlement possessed two factors that promoted the propagation of Protestantism. The first was a local community of African and diasporic Christians. The second was a large community especially receptive to the new faith. This group included numerous freed slaves after 1808, when Sierra Leone became the site at which victims of the Atlantic slave trade were freed by British naval vessels that seized them under the 1807 anti–slave trade act. The freed slaves, many of whom converted, rapidly became the most successful Christian "missionaries" in Africa. By the 1860s thousands of them had returned to their homelands, especially Yorubaland, bringing their faith with them. Most operated under the guidance of the Church Missionary Society's "native pastorage" rules, which meant that they still acknowledged the authority of English bishops and kept quite close to European Protestant doctrines. Others, however, began to integrate Christian ideas and practices into local religion. Yet, despite this influx of African missionaries, conversion in West Africa remained relatively slow before 1850. The potential for wealth, status, and institutional advancement that conversion offered was balanced by the problems of Christian exclusivity and the popularity of local cosmologies and faiths. It would take several decades for locals to find ways to balance these faiths in West Africa.

Southern Africa was not as connected to the Sierra Leone network, but here too it was African missionaries who did much of the work of spreading evangelical Christianity. To be sure, European missionaries contributed. Most of these were Protestants. While a few Portuguese and Italian Catholics remained in West Africa, the rush of Protestant missionaries into the southern half of the continent in the nineteenth century was unprecedented. In East Africa, Johann Ludwig Krapf of the Church Missionary Society arrived in Mombasa in 1844, followed by other Basel and CMS missionaries who established missions deep in the interior. Many of these were Britons such as the famous Scots David Livingstone and John MacKenzie and Englishmen like William Tozer. By 1882, they would even reach the deep interior states of Buganda and the Lozi kingdom. Nevertheless, they found few Africans willing to become Christian, and it was the first generation of local converts who found ways to make Protestant scripts and practices understandable and useful to locals. The most important of these was Dallington Scopion Maftaa, a Zanzibari who translated the Bible into Swahili with the help of a local Muslim scribe and who served as the first permanent missionary in Buganda.

In southern Africa, Protestantism was first brought by the seventeenth-century Dutch settlers, most of whom were Calvinists. Yet they did not evangelize Africans in this early period, and formal Christianity held little attraction for the Khoi-speaking people of the region. Only in the mid–eighteenth century were missionary activities undertaken among the larger communities where Khoi-speaking and isiXhosa-speaking Africans mixed and mingled with immigrants from Asia and Europe. It was in these groups that some concepts and practices from Christianity began to spread. Among the important agents in this respect was Adam Kok, a former slave in Cape Town who purchased his own freedom and then led his followers into the colony's interior. Kok and his followers adopted a number of Christian practices, and his descendants helped to build the London Missionary Society station in Klaarwater in 1801. A second generation included Jager Afrikaner, a Khoi-speaker who was captain, or leader, of a multilingual community on the edges of European lands in the early nineteenth century. A charismatic leader, he had a vision of God that led him to personally embrace Christianity. Many of his followers also at least nominally accepted the faith. Yet overall, Dutch Calvinism did not spread widely in the region. It was only the late eighteenth-century arrival of Moravian missionaries in the Eastern Cape that led to massive conversions among Khoi-speakers and isiXhosa-speakers. These converts were at least partly attracted by the skills and opportunities the missionaries provided and the protection they offered from harsh treatment by the Dutch-speaking settlers. Soon after, missionaries from the London Missionary Society also arrived. These missionaries' values of justice and "free will" often earned them the enmity of European settlers. For example, LMS missionary James Read encouraged Khoi servants to take their masters to court for abuse or cruelty and as a result was criticized by the European community in which he served. This ethic was only one reason that the LMS missionaries won converts. They also expanded their flock by marrying Khoi-speaking or other local wives. Yet these missionary groups were not entirely egalitarian. Even their own children and other local followers whom they helped to become preachers and missionaries were often unpaid and unrecognized by their missionary societies. Disgruntled, these locals often became leaders in adapting Christianity for local consumption outside of the strict rules and power structures of the missionaries, as we will see later.

In this period Christian innovation was also taking place in Ethiopia, where Abyssinian Christianity was entering a period of intense theological debate. The eighteenth century and early nineteenth century in Ethiopia were an era in which the state was relatively weak and local warlords fought each other for power and influence. These nobles and their factions also held different conceptions of the incarnations of Christ. The Ethiopian church generally held that Christ had been both divine and human in life, but in death the human incarnation was absorbed into the divine. However, in this period both the nature of Christ and the question of how to honor the Sabbath came to be challenged, and both monasteries and their benefactors chose various sides. Nor was this the only threat to the Abyssinian church. The expansion of neighboring Muslim states and the entrance of Protestant missionaries sponsored by the Church Missionary Society in 1830 also challenged the church. The Protestants were initially accepted but later created problems by trying to "purify" Christianity of local folk practices like worshiping saints, kissing the cross, and keeping fasts. This challenge to local doctrine and practice was only to be overcome when, in the late 1850s, Emperor Tewodros reunified the state and reasserted its control over the church.

The Xhosa Cattle Killing

As the preceding sections illustrate, the religious experiences of Africans in the eighteenth and nineteenth centuries were highly diverse, and it is difficult to represent them in a single example. However, the encounters of the Xhosa-speaking peoples of southern Africa with evangelical Protestantism help to illustrate some of the ways in which Africans strove to understand, assimilate, and make use of new spiritual ideas and practices filtering in from other parts of the continent and the wider world during this period.

As we saw in chapter 1, the political and cultural stability of eighteenth-century Xhosa society was a result of the carefully-constructed balance between the power and authority of neighborhood leaders, chiefs, and kings, all of whom had various roles in rites of passage and communal imaginations like the veneration of cattle. This balance helped to integrate new members and overcome challenges to the community. However, the system was seriously challenged by a series of wars of European expansion beginning around 1779. In these conflicts, first Dutch-speaking settlers and then English-speakers fought to seize land previously controlled by the Xhosa. As a result, by 1820, Xhosa society had lost control of vast tracts of land. Some had been transferred directly to settlers, and other territories and their inhabitants had been placed under the "indirect" rule of British magistrates.

In the settler-dominated territories, large areas of land were transformed from small family plots and communally owned pastoral grasslands into private sheep ranches producing wool for British factories. Over several decades, British governors slowly broke down the institutions of Xhosa society within these territories. Under a series of new laws, chiefs were

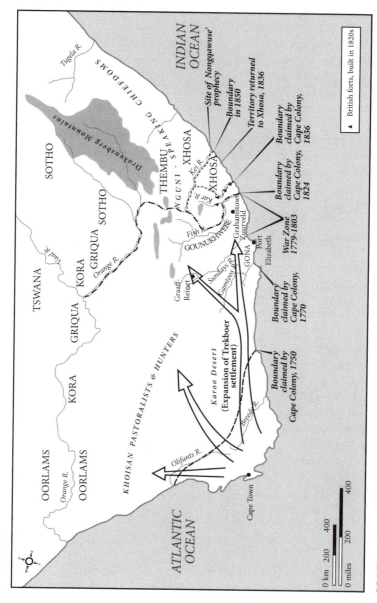

MAP 5   European expansion and the Xhosa, 1750–1850

forced to break up their households, young men were put to work building roads, and children were sent to Christian mission schools. Yet the greatest impact resulted not from new laws but from a new disease. In the mid–nineteenth century, European settlers mistakenly imported bovine pneumonia (or lung sickness). By 1855, this disease was killing Xhosa cattle at the rate of 5,000 head a month. Another disease affecting the staple maize (corn) crop broke out around the same time.

Meanwhile, some Xhosa still lived in technically independent states, the largest of which was the kingdom known as Gcalekaland. Even this state, however, was deeply affected by the epidemics. Crowded onto smaller and less fertile plots of land by an influx of refugees from the directly ruled territories, the Gcaleka citizens similarly suffered from losses of cattle and crops. This was not only an economic issue but also a deeply social one. As we have seen, for Xhosa, cattle served as social as well as financial capital. Wealth in cattle meant social status, and for men adulthood was partly proved by possession of cattle. Cattle were transferred from a man's family to a woman's in cases of marriage, and lawsuits (including for adultery or sexual transgressions) were settled through payments of cattle as well. Without cattle, the whole social structure of society was in danger of breaking down.

Nongqawuse and her fellow prophetess, Nonkosi, posed by British colonial police following their capture, c. 1858

It was during this crisis that a fifteen-year-old woman named Non-gqawuse went down to her family's maize fields on the Gxarha River in Qol-ora, where her job was to chase away the birds. On this day, together with her cousin Nonkosi, she heard voices coming from the river. Two strangers introduced themselves as Sifubasibanzi (wide-chest) and Napakade (for-ever). Only Nongqawuse seemed to be able to communicate with them. They told Nongqawuse to tell her uncle Mhlakaza that he must convey a message from the other world. The message was that the Xhosa should kill their cattle and stop cultivating their crops. If this was done, on a said day the ancestors would return with cattle and food and help to drive the Euro-pean settlers out. One oral source collected in the 1880s relates the words of Napakade as follows:

> "You are to tell the people that the whole community is to rise again from the dead. Then go on to say to them that all the cattle living now must be slaughtered, for they are reared with defiled hands, as the people handle witchcraft. Say to them there must be no ploughing of land, rather must the people dig deep pits (granaries), erect new huts, set up wide, strongly built cattlefolds, make milksacks, and weave doors from buka roots. The people must give up witchcraft on their own, not waiting until they are exposed by the witchdoctors. You are to tell them that these are the words of their chiefs—the words of Napakade and Sifubasibanzi" (pp. 70–71)

Mhlakaza immediately began to proselytize this message to his neighbors and to destroy his own crops and cattle. Although many Xhosa were skeptical, the ruler of Gcalekaland, Sarhili, was converted into a believer in July 1856, and he used his influence to convince many of his chiefly officeholders and advisers to do the same. Even many Xhosa living under direct colonial rule joined in.

This "cattle-killing" episode has been interpreted in many ways: as a response to environmental collapse, as evidence of women's dissatisfaction with the breakdown of social protections for wives and girls, and as a rebel-lion against European influence. Each of these explanations seems to have some validity. However, as historian J. B. Pieres points out, the story is not complete without an understanding of the spiritual world of the local popula-tion. Xhosa religion around 1750 held a deep ambivalence toward death. The ancestors were venerated, but death was also evil and feared, especially following a smallpox epidemic in 1770. In fact, Xhosa-speakers often aban-doned the homesteads where ancestors had died and moved to new areas. When Christian missionaries began to preach among the Xhosa, they found that the messages of heaven and of resurrection within their liturgy and the Bible attracted great attention, perhaps as a way to resolve the ambiva-lence toward death. Indeed, this particular set of ideas was quickly adapted by Xhosa prophets such as Nxele and Ntsikina in the 1820s. Nxele apparently included the Christian stories of creation, the flood, and crucifixion in his attack on "witchcraft." He claimed to be born from Mary, the mother of Christ. Later, he preached that the ancestors would return to "put right" the world in an adaptation of the resurrection idea within Christianity.

Pieres believes that the cattle-killing movement of the 1850s was born of the same Christian theology. He argues that the overcrowding of Gcalekaland following the European expansion meant that people could no longer move away from the homesteads of the dead. Building on Nxele's message, groups of mission-trained Xhosa reinterpreted resurrection in the form of the apocalyptic "end of days" that was featured in the Bible. This apocalyptic prediction, Pieres argues, was present in the story Nongqawuse told of her meeting with Napakade and Sifubasibanzi. In fact, he argues, the two represent God (the father) and Christ, with traditional Khoi and Xhosa names for gods imposed on Christian deities.

Pieres goes further, arguing that Mhlakaza was himself a disgruntled former Christian (Methodist, later Anglican) convert and something of a lay preacher who had gone by the name of Wilhelm Goliath. Goliath had worked with the archdeacon Nathaniel Merriman in the 1840s before being dismissed following a dispute with Merriman's wife. If Goliath and Mhlakaza were in fact the same person, the route of transmission of Christian ideas of the apocalypse and resurrection into Nongqawuse' prophecy would be explained. Several scholars have disputed the connection, arguing that Goliath was reported to be living in another district. However, the personal identity of Mhlakaza is not that important, since, as we have seen, the resurrection story had already been adapted by Xhosa prophets to their needs for decades prior to Nongqawuse. While European missionaries had first introduced the ideas, the key actors in this process were Africans—prophets and mission-educated fighters who had not meekly "accepted Christianity" but rather Africanized it to help make sense of a changing world. I will return to discuss the implications of this movement for the economic stability and political independence of the Xhosa community in the next chapter.

REFERENCES

African "World" and African "Traditional" Religions
Ikenga-Metuh, Emefie. *Comparative Studies of African Traditional Religions* (Onitsha: IMICO, 1987).

Isichei, Elizabeth. *The Religious Traditions of Africa: A History* (Westport: Praeger, 2004).

African Islam in the Eighteenth Century
Hiskett, Mervyn. *The Course of Islam in Africa* (Edinburgh: Edinburgh University Press, 1994).

Levtzion, Nehemia, and Randall L. Pouwels, eds. *The History of Islam in Africa* (Athens: Ohio University Press, 2000).

African Christianity and Protestant Evangelism
Isichei, Elizabeth. *A History of Christianity in Africa: From Antiquity to Present* (Lawrenceville: Africa World Press, 1995).

Kalu, Ogbu U. *African Christianity: An African Story* (Trenton, NJ: Africa World Press, 2007).

The Xhosa Cattle Killing
Gqoba, William. "The Cause of the Cattle-Killing at the Nongqause Period." Translated by A. C. Jordan in *Towards an African Literature: The Emergence of Literary Form in Xhosa* (Berkeley: University of California Press, 1973), 70–75.

Pieres, J. B. *The Dead Will Arise, Nongqawuse and the Great Xhosa Cattle-Killing Movement of 1856–7* (Johannesburg: Ravan Press, 1989).

African Economies and the Industrial Revolution

PRODUCTION AND PRODUCTIVITY IN LATE EIGHTEENTH-CENTURY AFRICA

In 1750, much of the world was engaged in a commercial boom that had been slowly building over the previous four centuries. Vast fleets of Asian vessels connected the dense populations of India, China, Arabia, and Indonesia while European galleys shipped raw materials and precious metals from the Americas to the old-world continents and returned full of people and finished products. Some trading routes spanned the globe, beginning in Europe and crossing the equator before heading south-east around the Cape of Good Hope at the southern tip of Africa or alternately south-west the Cape of Storms in Latin America before pushing north again to the great trading ports of Manila in the Philippines, Guangzhou in China, and Malacca in Southeast Asia.

Africans participated in this global commerce as traders, consumers, and sailors. Of course, the best-known story of Africans in transcontinental trade for this period is that of the Atlantic slave trade, the principal topic of volume 1 in this series. Beginning around 1450, this commerce in humans was still massive in scale by the late eighteenth century and impacted Africa deeply. Yet by 1850, it had largely come to an end, whereas African participation in other large-scale commercial ventures was on the increase. In the intervening years, the industrial revolution in Great Britain had begun to massively transform global trading patterns, and Africans had acted to master the new challenges wrought by the industrial revolution and take advantage of the possibilities it created.

Yet the story of economic production in eighteenth-century Africa is not just one of long-distance trade. Africans produced tools, foodstuffs, and goods to meet the needs of their own households and their nearby neighbors as well as faraway consumers. Overwhelmingly, such goods were produced through the shared labor of members of households with help from the wider extended family. Food production, especially, was most often a family affair. Sometimes, particular members of the family were responsible for specific crops or types of livestock. Often this division of labor was gendered, with men and women working separately. Some work was also reserved for the very young and very old. Children were assigned to keep pests away from crops and to watch livestock, for example, while the elderly were often involved in processing grains at the house. Often, however, the cultivation of staple crops was the responsibility of the family as a whole. In places where short periods of intense land preparation or harvesting were required, this meant not only the household but also members of the extended family. Some scholars believe that this need for intense labor in clearing fields or harvesting crops may have helped to develop the types of extended family structures common in large parts of eighteenth-century Africa. In such areas, the need to mobilize labor quickly and effectively was met by the development of clans. The assimilative natures of many of these clan structures and their readiness to absorb strangers as fictive kin also may have been aimed at addressing labor needs.

Other social institutions besides the clan may also have been oriented toward increasing communal production of goods. Young members of many secret societies, like the Poro men's society among the Senufo of West Africa, conducted labor in community fields and learned the values of hard work in the field as part of their initiation. Similarly, the trend toward age regiments of young men among the Nguni-speaking peoples of southern Africa, such as the BaSotho and BaTswana, may have helped to mobilize labor for irrigation and other projects needed for cultivation.

In many African societies, moreover, local political institutions played some role in production, often in return for taxes or tribute.

These payments were often lucrative and ritual at the same time. They could include "first fruits"—the right to the first portion of a harvest—or more extensive taxes. In the eighteenth century, taxes in some societies were quite exploitative. Ethiopia's ruling class, for example, extracted labor, services, *and* a share of all produce from workers they ruled over. At the same time, social systems in place in most areas acted to limit this kind of extraction. We saw, for example, that the moral code of Kongo threatened the greedy with punishment as witches. Other ways of limiting extraction included shared rules of rights of inheritance, like the guarantee against land alienation that most Ethiopian peasants enjoyed. Still others included ways of convincing the wealthy to redistribute some of their wealth to the poor. Among many Igbo-speaking communities, for example, the rise to noble rank involved paying initiation fees to society, holding feasts, and even giving away goods.

Ruling groups and individuals frequently also provided safety for merchants and sponsored markets for the sale of goods. They did so by exerting both military/political power and ritual authority. In major Igbo-speaking communities, for example, groups of local nobles ensured that markets were considered neutral spaces by creating both a special court of the market and a market god to watch over it. In return, they received certain ritual financial fees. As we will see, however, some of these institutions had broken down by the eighteenth century in areas particularly affected by the global slave trade.

While greed was often discouraged, entrepreneurship was encouraged in various ways within African societies. One type of entrepreneur was the rural pioneer who turned an area of wilderness into a farm. Usually, these entrepreneurs were rewarded by having some particular right acknowledged. One example comes from Kikuyu society, which in the early nineteenth century was based in the central highlands of what is today Kenya but spreading into new areas through assimilation, intermarriage, and the movement of groups of people to areas otherwise unoccupied by agrarian communities. Individuals who moved to new territory and cleared it for cultivation were considered pioneers and had the right of "first clearing," which meant they owned the land, although it could not be sold without the family agreeing. Groups that moved onto the land later were usually required to pay some sort of rent or tribute. This could be a significant financial payment in plant and animal products or a largely ritual transfer of first fruits. Moreover, these latecomers had less right to stay on the land and could be called upon for labor at times.

In addition to individual entrepreneurs, groups of Africans also formed large trading concerns or corporations. Sometimes, as among some Igbo-speaking communities, the whole community might serve as a corporation owning and benefiting from a marketplace. Usually, the corporations were somewhat related to extended real or fictive family structures. The Aro network in southern Nigeria, for example, was made up of Igbo-speakers like many of their neighbors, but its members defined themselves as an identity group stressing their own individual identities. They promoted intermarriage for their men but also tried to keep their women from marrying out of the group in order to promote family unity. By the late eighteenth century, the Aro had built a grid of markets served by a trade network tapping into specialists across the region. They even built movable trade fairs that traveled around the countryside. Other trade networks like the Mande Dyula network stressed their individuality through their Islamic identity. In East Africa, a web of trade networks tied the Swahili-speaking Zanzibari to groups of the interior. Some, like the Nywamwezi, organized partnerships to control trade routes and markets linking to the Zanzibari.

We can see, therefore, that most production in Africa in this period was organized along family or corporate lines. In some cases, specialized production was also associated with some sort of apprenticeship or special social status. Workshops associated with textile, leather, and metal production especially were frequently run by master craftspeople who employed a number of apprentices. Often, and especially in urban North Africa, all the workshops within a region were organized along the lines of a guild, with regulations for individuals hoping to move upward from apprentice to journeyman and finally master. However, even these guilds were often remarkably domestic, situated in or near the master craftsperson's home and largely introducing family members as apprentices. Some trade were so highly wrapped up with lineage systems that they took on the appearance of castes, with professions passed on from parent to child and the specialist group limited in its ability to intermarry with other members of the community and subject to certain taboos. Within Wolof society in Senegambia, such hereditary classes of artisans included leatherworkers (*uude*), knowledge professionals like the griot performer/historians (*gewel*), and blacksmiths (*tegg*).

Slavery was another mode by which labor was organized in some parts of eighteenth-century Africa, although it was still relatively rare outside of urban North Africa and a few coastal regions of West and East Africa connected to long-distance slave trades. In fact, the type of unfree labor present even in these regions was generally quite different from the chattel slavery through which labor was organized on plantations in some parts of Asia and the Americas. Instead, some African entrepreneurs and families employed a wide range of dependents who were not free to leave and who did not have full status as free members of society but who had a number of rights guaranteed by law or religion. Often, these unfree laborers could become free peasants or full family members over time, and in most cases they worked alongside family members rather than in large gangs. Only in a few regions was slave labor the main component of local production in this period, for example, in some parts of Sudan and Egypt and perhaps along a stretch of the Senegal River Valley.

However they were produced, most African goods were consumed locally by households and their neighbors. Nevertheless, there was also in this period extensive long-distance trade both within the continent and across to Europe, Asia, and the Americas. Merchants and producers engaged in these networks of exchange used various sorts of currency. In some cases, barter was the system of exchange of choice. However, there were also widespread African currencies like the *umumu*, or iron knives produced by Igbo smiths and copper bangles. These were desired largely for the intrinsic value of the metal of which they were composed. Imported currency was often valued for both its intrinsic worth and its rarity. European and Asian coins, as well as locally produced coinage, were in circulation across northern Africa in 1750. In fact, metallic coins from the Spanish mines in the Americas had been coming into Africa so fast in the preceding century that they had led to a great decline in the value of certain metals. Another currency in wide usage was the cowry shell, imported from Asia, which was used across wide swaths of central and western Africa in the eighteenth century. Finally, textiles were in high demand both as a trade good and as currency.

In the mid–eighteenth century, the economic situation in much of coastal Africa and even deep into the interior had been significantly shaped by the expanding trade in enslaved humans that had characterized the previous several centuries. The Atlantic slave trade, especially, reached its height in the 1760s, with approximately 80,000 Africans enslaved and exported per annum. Africans were also forced to cross the Indian Ocean in this period at captives, probably at about half the rate of the Atlantic trade. The transoceanic leg of this slave trade was largely operated by traders based in the Arabian Peninsula and the Horn of Africa. At the same time, a number of sub-Saharan Africans were also enslaved as laborers in North Africa. The regions most affected by slaving during this period were the Bight of Benin (modern-day southwestern Nigeria) and Angola, but Madagascar, Sudan, Mozambique, and the Horn of Africa were also extensively victimized in this period.

The most intensive of these trades, the Atlantic slave trade, arguably affected population levels and productivity in these regions, as well as in areas of West Africa that had earlier been major hunting grounds for slavers. Historians like Patrick Manning and Tiyambe Zeleza have estimated that African populations stagnated overall in the eighteenth century, and although some scholars disagree, it seems likely that specific regions like Madagascar, Mozambique, and the Bight of Benin probably experienced appreciable demographic decline. Moreover, the slave trade probably affected productivity for a number of reasons beyond population levels. Slavers tended to claim the most productive members of society, the slave trade caused famines and wars, and the threat of slave raiding forced people to relocate to inaccessible but defensible sites far away from their fields and major trade routes. It is no surprise that many West African towns founded in this period were on stilts in swamps or deep in mountains and forests.

Moreover, the Atlantic slave trade was accompanied by an expansion of imported manufactured goods including weapons, textiles, and metalcrafts. These began to flow into the continent, and in so doing replaced locally produced goods. For example, the bark cloth produced in Kongo was slowly replaced by imported Indian and then British cotton textiles. As this happened, Africans in this region took the first steps away from manufacturing sufficient goods to meet their needs and toward producing raw materials and consuming manufactured goods produced elsewhere. At the same time, this trade also realigned commercial routes so that local trade broke down in some regions of Africa to be replaced by imports from Europe and Asia.

In some areas, the commercial realities of the Atlantic Ocean and Indian Ocean slave trades led to significant socioeconomic reconfigurations. Most dramatic was the rise of vampire states, political entities that survived by exporting their own populations. The Lunda state that rose in Central Africa around the 1750s was an example of this. As this state expanded, its armies enslaved entire regions and exchanged the captives for goods manufactured in Europe and Asia. Other states merely incorporated slave trading into economies that were also involved in production of raw materials and finished products. The Asante kings, for example, extracted captives as tribute from their northern conquests and sent them to the coast for sale to Europeans, although this trade remained secondary in importance to the Kola trade in this period. In an effort to control the entirety of the route to the coast and extract fees from each stage of the process, the Asante kings sought to control the coast, most notably through an invasion of the main Gold Coast ports in 1807. Similarly, the kings of Dahomey sought to dominate coastal slave-trading ports like Whydah and Allada, especially in the Badagri wars of 1783–1784.

Whether operating through corporations like the Aro trading community or states like Asante and Dahomey, the slave trade in the eighteenth century was often highly organized. However, it also frequently caused a great deal of chaos, including (as we have seen) civil war in Kongo. The extension of the slave trade to Mozambique and southeast Africa has even been advanced as a major cause of the *mfecane*, the massive movement of peoples in the region that led to widespread warfare but also caused the coalescing of identities such as that of the Zulu. However, this great movement was probably the result of several other major transformations, as we will see.

Although it is difficult to quantify, it is clear the international trade in captives had a major impact on Africa. After about 1810, however, the Atlantic slave trade began to decline in scope. This was partly a result of legal abolition of the slave trade by the main European and American countries involved in it. Denmark was the first European state to forbid its citizens to trade in slaves with a law that took effect in 1803. However, it was abolition by Britain, the main power involved in the slave trade, that really began the process by which the trade diminished. British abolitionism emerged as a movement in the 1780s, spurred on partly by the writings of Africans of the diaspora like Olaudah Equiano (Gustuvas Vassa). Their narratives of suffering and redemption were received by a middle-class British audience that was receptive to them for several political and cultural reasons. The first was that the British middle class were already engaged in a domestic political struggle against aristocrats, many of whom were owners of slave plantations. Abolitionism was thus partly a tool by which they could strike a blow against political enemies. Another reason was that abolitionism merged with important ideas of free labor and personal redemption within the evangelical Christianity espoused by this class. Finally, the slave trade interfered with many British merchants' attempts to extract other resources from Africa, and thus these merchants rapidly became leading abolitionists. Spurred on by all these motivations, the middle-class abolitionists carried out a campaign to win the support of lower-class members of society, and especially women, through a public relations effort that forced the British Parliament to criminalize the trade in 1807. Enforcement of the ban was uneven, but nevertheless the number of captives enslaved in Africa declined rapidly.

AFRICANS AND THE INDUSTRIAL REVOLUTION

The abolition of the Atlantic slave trade was closely tied to a deeper transformation in global economics in the late eighteenth and early nineteenth centuries. This was the first industrial revolution, which began in Britain and gradually spread to other parts of Europe and the world. At its heart, the industrial revolution was an energy revolution, one in which mechanized factories utilizing coal and steam power gradually replaced biological forms of energy in the production of goods. Yet it was much more than that. The industrial revolution transformed social systems as it uprooted farmers from their land and turned them into factory workers. It reoriented the trading systems of the world and put economic power in the hands of a relative few in northeastern Europe. It promoted new systems of thought and valued capitalist accumulation and innovation over balance and tradition. Rather rapidly, its effects were felt in well-separated areas of the globe, including parts of Africa.

The origins of the industrial revolution are a complex topic, but several factors can be identified in eighteenth-century Britain and in its relationship to the world that helped to catalyze its beginning. Certainly one precondition was the agricultural revolution, a package of new crops imported from the Americas and new practices for growing foodstuffs that emerged in Britain and the Netherlands in the seventeenth century. This package helped the British to turn large areas of land over to production of surplus goods for processing and sale, rather than just growing sufficient food to sustain their population. Another precondition was the local prevalence of easily mined coal. Britain has numerous coal seams close to the surface and often close to good transportation routes like rivers, allowing the coal to be shipped around the country quite easily and inexpensively. Moreover, Britain had already begun to move toward a political and legal system that favored individual accumulation of wealth. The British Parliament included many merchants and producers even prior to the eighteenth century, and they helped to make laws spurring on industrial development, often at great cost to the unrepresented peasants who were turned off their land to become factory workers.

In addition, the industrial revolution was greatly stimulated by Britain's overseas colonies and commercial settlements. By harvesting raw materials and foods from the Caribbean, Africa, and North America, Britain was able to divert its own labor force to industrial production. Diasporic Africans contributed by producing vast amounts of calories—in the form of sugar—as well as other goods for British workers. At the same time, financing was available to British industrialists from profits derived from the international opium trade dominated by Britain in Asia, as well as the Atlantic slave trade.

Continental Africans, as well, contributed decisively to the development of the British industrial revolution. Their main contribution was primarily in three areas. The first was the production of primary resources such as cotton and wool, which fed the factories of Britain. The second was industrial materials, including lubricants and gums that were used in the production process. The third was crops consumed by European workers and managers, such as coffee, tea, spices, and tobacco. In addition, North Africans in this period produced foodstuffs for the European market that may have helped France to enter the industrial age in the early nineteenth century.

Probably the most important of these goods were indigenous oilseeds that provided lubricants and lighting for factories and industrial facilities. Palm oil, produced in tropical regions of the world but especially West Africa, was one of these. Palm oil was used for candles, for industrial lubrication, and also for making soap—a necessity in the grimy industrial age. In areas where oil palms grew well and easy transportation was available, palm oil quickly became the product of choice for African exporters. Thus whereas Britain imported only 223 tons of palm oil from West Africa in 1800, the country took in 10,673 tons thirty years later, and twice that (21,723 tons) in 1850.

Much of this palm oil came from the Niger River delta, which had the perfect conditions for growing oil palms as well as a preexisting transportation network along the river itself. Most of the producers here were families who owned their own land and sold to merchants who transported the oil and palm kernels down the river. In return, the producers imported large amounts of luxury goods from Europe, including crops. In a few areas, like some regions of the Gold Coast, some plantations may have been worked by slaves, but in general palm oil production was the job of extended families and perhaps some sharecroppers.

Another oil crop that grew in popularity in this period was the groundnut, or peanut. Groundnuts grew well in slightly drier areas such as Senegambia. They were used locally as a foodstuff, but the oil they contained also became popular in Europe during this period for cooking, lubrication, soap, and illuminating oil. Farmers in the Guinea region began to export groundnuts and then groundnut oil in the 1820s, but the crop only really took off in the 1840s, when the people of the Senegal River area began to cultivate it in great quantities. In 1835, only 47 tons of groundnuts were exported to Europe. By 1851, this had become 11,095 tons.

In Senegambia and the Niger River delta area, the transition to long-distance trade in industrial materials and primary resources was relatively rapid and successful. In other areas, the prohibition of the transatlantic slave trade caused something of an economic crisis. This was especially true in areas where there were no apparent desirable raw materials or where the cost of transporting goods to the coast was especially high. It was also true, however, in some areas where there was a desirable local resource. In southeast Africa, for example, the prohibition of the slave trade led some slaving groups to turn to harvesting ivory for the global market. Ivory was in great demand as an industrial middle class rose in Europe, not least because the piano (with its ivory keys) quickly became a mark of status. Around the turn of the century, therefore, elephant hunting became a large-scale competitive business in Mozambique and surrounding areas. This helped to reinforce the "big man" system of politics in the area that had developed around men who had led slave raids. Through both slave trading and later ivory trading, these self-made chiefs earned luxury goods that they distributed to their followers in order to keep their loyalty. However, the demand for ivory quickly led to the virtual extinction of elephants, which in turn led to increased competition and sometimes outright warfare among the chiefs and their followers. This may have been exacerbated by periodic droughts that wracked the region in the 1810s. It has been suggested that it was this combination, rather than the slave trade, that caused the *mfecane* of the 1810s and 1820s discussed in the preceding section.

While Africans became integrated in various ways into the new industrial economy, it has been argued that their participation as producers of raw materials did not help advance their own continent economically. One of the earliest scholarly texts to place African experiences in the context of the first industrial revolution was the Afro-Caribbean scholar Walter Rodney's *How Europe Underdeveloped Africa* (1972). Rodney and those who came after him point out that Africa in that period and ever since largely produced raw materials but consumed finished products, and that most of the profit from this cycle thus ended up in the industrialized nations of Europe, North

America, and increasingly Asia. In their view, global industrialization has exacerbated poverty and caused massive environmental damage in Africa and was a major enabling factor in the conquest and colonial rule of African states by outsiders.

At the same time, some evidence suggests that many African producers and merchants were in fact very successful in creating wealth through trading with Europeans. Most of the production that took place was in the hands of African peasants and family producers, who used the profits to increase their personal and familial wealth. In some areas, in fact, mid-nineteenth-century Africans were able to play European merchants against each other to set the prices they wanted for their goods. It is even possible to suggest that it was this success that led Europeans to invade Africa in the late nineteenth century in order to control production and prices themselves. This, however, is an argument for volume 3 of this series.

SETTLERS, PEASANTS, AND PLANTATIONS

The transition to producing raw materials and industrial lubricants and soaps could have been expected to impact African labor patterns, and indeed it did. However, the ways in which this happened were determined to a significant degree not only by global conditions but also by Africans' own strategies for mastering the new global production and commercial patterns. Like producers everywhere, Africans strove to control prices and to produce goods that brought the greatest profit. Both peasants and large-scale landowners sought to maximize their own and often their families' and societies' benefits from the trade. At the same time, however, European and especially British merchants competed to keep benefits in their own hands. Africans also had to compete against their neighbors and against producers elsewhere in the world. They met with varying results in this effort.

One set of areas in which production styles changed the most and Africans benefited the least were regions where European settlers took over production and ran their farms and ranches along capitalist lines. This was relatively new in Africa. Even in the Cape of Good Hope, European wine and grain farmers of the seventeenth and eighteenth centuries had tended to run their farms through a slave mode of production rather than on a truly capitalist model, drawing in laborers brought from Malaysia or Indonesia or captured in battles with Khoi, Xhosa, and BaSotho groups. Indeed, the demand for slaves among these European farmers and Euro-African communities that grew up near them may have been one more long-term underlying cause of the *mfecane* that rocked southern Africa in the 1810s and 1820s. Even in the 1830s, when slavery technically became illegal in the Cape Colony under British law, most settler farmers only superficially transitioned their labor system. They largely turned to paying their laborers "in kind"—food, housing, and even alcohol—rather than with wages, and these laborers had to stay because they found relatively few other opportunities to pursue an independent lifestyle within or outside of the colony.

It was the arrival of large numbers of British immigrants in the Eastern Cape in 1820 that added a layer of settler capitalism on top of this system. The settlers were mostly urban Englishmen and a few Scots who had been lured by promisess of land and were given a broad swath of territory on the eastern edge of the colony. This land had been recently seized from the Xhosa, and the British governor of the colony hoped that the settlers would serve as a buffer between the Afrikaners of the colony and the Xhosa, and would also produce wool that could be sent to British factories and would provide a taxable export for the colony. The settlers soon discovered that they needed a great deal of labor and also came to desire yet more land, and they therefore called for the expansion of the colony to annex Xhosa territory and to turn the remaining independent Xhosa into laborers rather than free farmers. Although some administrators did not support this effort, over the next thirty-five years or so most of the territory of the Xhosa was annexed by the colony.

The settlers, and the missionaries and administrators around them, largely supported a system of capitalist labor in which the laborers were paid wages, although often these were insufficient. Land-owning settlers set up recruitment camps in Xhosa territory, collecting potential laborers looking for cash. In some cases, these may have been captives, but most simply seem to have been forced into this arrangement because they had lost their land. Some were searching for a day-to-day subsistence, while others needed funds in order to marry. The new labor regime tended to concentrate these workers in "locations," segregated living quarters away from colonial towns but near enough to farms so as to serve as paid laborers. While not free to move around, often poorly treated, and definitely segregated, the laboring class here could be defined as wage laborers, thereby satisfying the moral demands of capitalist, "enlightened" European society. By the 1840s, such wage laborers made up a significant proportion of adult males among the Xhosa-speaking population of the Eastern Cape. Following the cattle-killing episode of the 1850s, a large number of impoverished Xhosa from within the independent Xhosa kingdom were forced to join their ranks, and soon thereafter the territory of the kingdom was annexed to the Cape Colony.

Wage labor also emerged in this period in Algeria, where following its 1830 invasion of the territory the French government tried to attract European settlers to grow sugarcane, coffee, silk, cotton, flax, tea, tobacco, and especially wheat and grapes for wine. Between 1830 and 1851, the French administrators turned lands previously controlled by the Algerian government over to settlers and soon added land taken from communities that they deemed to be unworthy of land-ownership or who revolted against French rule. As Europeans moved to control these farms, they often paid wages to their workers rather than granting them a portion of the crop or employing other models of labor.

Algeria and the Cape, however, are exceptions in this period. In general, settler capitalism failed in Africa in the period before 1875. Attempts by Portuguese farmers to grow cotton in Angola are a good example, failing spectacularly despite funding from the colonial administration. Why did settler capitalism not work? There are at least four reasons. First, in much of Africa the demographic impact of the Atlantic slave trade had led to a scarcity of labor. This scarcity was exacerbated by the second factor, Africans' unwillingness to work on plantations for wages. African laborers generally preferred to try to find their own land or to work under a sharecropping or other system in which profits were somehow shared. Moreover, this was a period in which commodity prices rose and fell rapidly. Large wage-paying plantations simply could not switch the crops they produced rapidly enough to adjust to these permutations. Third, plantation models and methods of production imported from Europe were often much less efficient given local soil and environmental conditions than were local methods of production. This led to lower yields on big plantations than the peasant producer with which they competed could produce. Finally, local regimes and institutions often resisted the imposition of settlers and their systems of labor quite successfully. For example, a large system of French plantations imposed in the Senegal River Valley in 1818 failed in the face of resistance by the king of Waalo, local Islamic peasant organizations, and the Maures who controlled the territory across the river, all of whom saw the plantations as competitors.

Nevertheless, plantation agriculture did expand in Africa in the early nineteenth century, if not often run by European settlers and not often worked by wage labor. By the term "plantations," we mean large-scale agriculture employing gangs of workers, some of whom may have been enslaved, to produce surpluses for distribution or sale. In North Africa and parts of West and East Africa as well, plantations run under Islamic law especially expanded during this period. In many cases, these plantations were worked by unfree workers who had no right to leave but who enjoyed certain rights of manumission and conditions of treatment defined by Islamic law.

A West African example comes from the Sokoto Caliphate, about half of whose 20 million inhabitants were probably unfree and which produced many goods for local exchange and export, including agricultural foodstuffs, livestock, skins and hides, and ivory as well as textiles and ironware. In the 1820s, the caliphate had a large wealthy class and a legal and social system that supported ownership of large farms, as well as an economic system that could distribute their products. In some parts of the caliphate, particularly the regions of Kano and Katsina, these wealthy individual landowners and families seem to have employed hundreds of captive laborers to work their land, growing tobacco, shea nuts, cotton, indigo, sugarcane, and grains. In general, the workers were required to spend a certain proportion of their time working the plantation. They were also given some time to work their own plots, as well as food and housing. However, life was still quite harsh for these plantation laborers. They were supervised by taskmasters, some of whom were reportedly quite violent, and were housed separately from domestic laborers and the plantation owner.

In a few parts of East Africa, as well, an Islamic plantation system evolved in this time to provide spices and other commodities for the global trade network. These plantations were especially present in areas controlled by the Omani sultans of Zanzibar, in whose territories plantations were worked largely by immigrant laborers, including some war captives, serving as either sharecroppers or servile dependents. In the nineteenth century, the proportion of slave laborers on the plantations increased, especially on those that produced spices for the international trade. The plantations were privately owned and sometimes supported by the Busaidi sultans. More often, however, they were funded by Asian businessmen who advanced Swahili-speaking landowners the credit they needed to start their plantations and then bought the goods they produced at reduced rates. Here, too, workers labored under tough conditions but enjoyed some protections under Islamic law.

Non-Islamic plantations also emerged in western Africa around the same period. These included the *feitorias,* or peanut plantations, of Guinea, which were largely owned by creole descendants of Portuguese-speakers and their African wives. The laborers on these plantations were partly captives and partly contract laborers working on a debt system. The contract laborers were migrants who were given seed and tools for a price and a piece of land to work. Once they had repaid the debt for the seed and tools, anything left was theirs. However, because the landowner often set the price at which they would buy peanuts, only seldom was much profit left for the contract laborer. Another plantation type emerged in Madagascar in the 1820s, where the royal family gave members of the aristocracy and foreigners the title to large areas of land and to recruit local villagers to work for them for free for up to twenty-four days a year. This *fanompoana* system also spread to a number of Indian Ocean islands.

Overall, however, production in nineteenth-century Africa remained largely in the hands of free peasants, even in the production of the raw materials most in demand in the global market. Peanut cultivation in Senegal, for example, was carried out rather successfully by peasants who used the profits to arm themselves against interference both by their own governments and by Europeans. Palm oil in the Niger River delta and most of western Africa remained in the hands of small producers and was traded by small trading concerns and individuals. Even in Sudan, where the Egyptian government sought to create large plantations, these largely failed and were transformed into private individual smallholdings under state law, with peasants taxed but producing for themselves.

What does this suggest for African economics in this period? Certainly the industrial revolution was bringing about change in African production and increasing African integration into the world economy. Some parts of Africa may have been barely touched by the changes, but overall their effects were felt widely. Yet Africans were not merely victims of this transformation. Rather, they seized upon multiple strategies to control and seek to benefit from the new economy. It has been previously incorrectly argued that their failure to do so indicated the weakness that made them ripe for colonialism in the late nineteenth century. However, it is also possible to argue that it was their success in profiting from the new global commerce in an environment of relatively free trade that eventually led Europeans to impose colonialism as a way to divert those profits into their own hands.

Muhammad Ali's Egypt

World histories generally reduce the role of Africans in the first decades of the industrial revolution to that of producers of raw materials and consumers of finished products. One extreme example of this is Egypt, which during the early nineteenth century became one of the world's leading producers of cotton and yet imported tons of finished cloth from Europe. However, the Egyptian case also proves the difficulties of overgeneralizing, since during this period Egypt also became a manufacturing power, although in the long term this sector of the economy did not thrive.

Eighteenth-century Ottoman Egypt had largely possessed an agricultural economy, producing food mostly for local consumption but also for export to neighbors. Cultivation techniques were determined by the flooding of the Nile River, which produced a single annual crop. Most of the productive land was owned by peasants, although some of it was in the hands of large landowners. In general, peasant producers had to pay very high levels of taxes to multiple groups—the state, the provincial governor, local headmen, tax-farmers who owned the right to take a percentage of all taxes, and even merchants and religious leaders. The tax burden was onerous, and peasants sometimes needed to protect themselves, by building their communities as fortresses, by ganging up on tax collectors, or periodically even by outright insurrection.

This system persisted throughout the eighteenth century despite some attempts at reform, the most significant of which was prompted by the French invasion of Egypt in 1798. Early French military successes made it clear to the Ottoman sultans and their governors in Egypt and elsewhere in North Africa that they needed to reform the government and military of the empire and its provinces. These reforms required cash, however, and it soon became clear that local peasant populations could not handle an additional tax burden. Moreover, the proposed reforms required the development of a class of officers and officials with significant expertise and access to modern military technology and weaponry, none of which was readily available in Egypt or other regions of the Ottoman Empire in this period.

In Egypt, this pattern of reform was largely undertaken in the late eighteenth century by the Mamluk, who administered the state for the Ottoman sultans. These military leaders attempted a number of reforms, which they tried to pay for with increased taxes, government monopolies, and tariffs on foreign trade. Each of these measures incited the resentment of segments of the Egyptian population without, however, producing any results. In the end it was only with the accession of the Albanian-born Muhammad

Ali to power in Egypt that a solution was found to break through this problem (see chapter 2). Ali managed to outflank potential opponents of reform first by massacring leading Mamluk officials in 1811 and second by putting tax collection back in the hands of the state rather than private tax-farmers. He recruited a loyal and effective class to manage this process consisting of not only well-trained government clerks but also local headmen. He then embarked on a three-part economic reform to support an expanded military and government.

The first stage in his reform of the Egyptian system of production was to stimulate the export of agricultural products, especially foodstuffs. Ali was helped in this by the conditions created in the Mediterranean region and Europe by the Napoleonic Wars. The Egyptian state was not only able to sell foodstuffs at high prices to British troops fighting the French in Egypt, but also to export food to Europe, where the war had raised prices overall. By declaring a state monopoly on the sale of grains, he was able to skim profits off the top of every transaction and to redirect these to the state.

Using these profits, Muhammad Ali then promoted the growth of profitable cash crops, especially cotton. Egyptian officials introduced cotton into the Nile River delta as a winter crop, grown in addition to grains rather than replacing them. Of course, this required peasants to work harder. Rather than resting during the off-season, they now had to labor year-round, and women and children were forced to join men in the fields. Moreover, the increase in production was only possible because of new irrigation projects, and these too had to be built by peasant laborers. All told, peasant families probably had to put in twice as many human-hours of work following the introduction of cotton as they had in previous decades. Yet the result of all this was a massive increase in Egyptian exports, especially in the second quarter of the century. Historian Roger Owen has estimated this increase as follows:

Estimate of the Volume of Egyptian Cotton Exports

PERIOD	AVERAGE ANNUAL VOLUME OF EXPORTS
1821–1825	124,252
1825–1829	186,641
1830–1834	180,610
1835–1839	228,939
1840–1844	195,653
1844–1849	236,392

The third step in the process of industrializing Egypt was to create a network of factories within the country to produce finished products. Muhammad Ali and his advisers recognized that the relegation of African societies to mere producers of raw materials left them economically dependent on Europe. Ali therefore moved in the 1820s to create a factory system in Egypt itself. He focused on the state, rather than individual entrepreneurs, as the main funding source and operator of these factories. The process began with the development of weapons factors and shipyards in Alexandria, through which the Egyptian government hoped to become militarily self-sufficient. Other factories processing foodstuffs and cotton were also initially developed to make uniforms and meals for the army. Soon, however, Ali's administration also began to build textile factories to deal with much of Egypt's cotton crop. Moreover, Ali insisted that Egyptians build the tools that operated in the factories, including looms, carding machines, and spinning jennies. Because Egypt did not possess sufficient coal to run all these machines on steam, some of these were animal powered. By the mid-1830s, Egyptian factories processed 20 percent of the cotton produced in the country.

Yet the Egyptian industrial sector faced a number of limitations. First, Egypt itself was a relatively small market, which meant that most of the goods produced there had to be exported. These goods often faced strict tariffs in Britain and throughout Europe that made it difficult to beat the prices of domestically produced goods. At the same time, Egypt was bound by a treaty between Britain and the Ottoman Empire and could not place tariffs on British textiles entering the country. Together, these two factors meant that Egyptian textiles had no markets in which they enjoyed a price advantage. Equally problematic, the lack of coal meant that Egypt had to import coal from Europe. This was prohibitively expensive and increased the price of goods produced in Egyptian factories.

Finally, the fluctuation of commodity prices in the mid–nineteenth century affected Egyptian cotton mills in a similar way as European plantations in Africa. When the price of cotton dropped in 1836, the Egyptian state found itself too reliant on proceeds from this single commodity and rapidly fell into debt. To pay those debts, the government tried to increase taxes on cotton farmers and to make money by selling cotton plantations to private individuals. These individuals, however, soon found they could profit more by selling their raw cotton on the open market rather than to the Egyptian state. By the 1840s, the result was a breakdown of both the rural taxation system and the state-centered factory system. Egypt's pathway to industrialization had ended, and European bankers owned high levels of Egyptian debt. As we will see in the next volume, this

Muhammad Ali with modern soldiers and Egyptian citizens, in front of the "sites" of Cairo. This picture, by a French artist, is meant to show the fusion of modern and ancient in Muhammad Ali's reign, 1841.

process helped pave the way for British occupation of Egypt in the late nineteenth century.

REFERENCES

Production and Productivity in Late Eighteenth-Century Africa
Manning, Patrick. *Slavery and African Life: Occidental, Oriental, and African Slave Trades* (Cambridge: Cambridge University Press, 1990).

Rodney, Walter. *How Europe Underdeveloped Africa* (Washington, DC: Howard University Press, 1981).

Africans and the Industrial Revolution
Inikori, Joseph E. *Africans and the Industrial Revolution in England: A Study in International Trade and Economic Development* (Cambridge: Cambridge University Press, 2002).

Law, Robin. *From Slave Trade to "Legitimate" Commerce: The Commercial Transition in Nineteenth-Century West Africa* (Cambridge: Cambridge University Press, 2002).

Settlers, Peasants, and Plantations
Lovejoy, Paul. "The Characteristics of Plantations in the Nineteenth-Century Sokoto Caliphate." *American Historical Review* 84 (1979): 1267–1292.

Zeleza, Tiyambe. *A Modern Economic History of Africa*. Vol. 1, *The Nineteenth Century* (Dakar: CODESRIA, 1993).

Muhammad Ali's Egypt
Issawi, Charles. *An Economic History of the Middle East and North Africa* (New York: Columbia University Press, 1982).

Owen, Roger. *The Middle East in the World Economy, 1800–1914* (New York: Methuen, 1981).

Africans Engage the West

MEN AND WOMEN IN THE MIDDLE?

The period covered in this volume is sandwiched between two giant and frequently-told stories of the African past—the era of the Atlantic slave trade and the coming of European colonial rule. In fact, it could be fairly argued that the period 1750–1875 in African history cannot be easily discussed without acknowledging the ongoing operation and impact of the transoceanic slave trades and the imminence of colonial invasion. This is especially true in a series like this one that seeks to discuss Africa in global perspective. It is for this reason that volumes 1 and 3 of this series focus on these themes.

This volume, however, focuses on the less well-known story of Africans' innovations, creativity, and adaptations to changes in their local and global environments in the eighteenth and nineteenth centuries. The central theme in this story is the cosmopolitanism of African societies, and the ways in which their social, economic, political, and cultural adaptability made possible rich existences and opportunities for locals, migrants, transients, and travelers to live together. This set of cosmopolitan lifestyles was not always harmonious, entirely egalitarian, or completely ecumenical. Yet it was one factor that explains the abilities of Africans in this period to survive and often thrive in an era of industrial capitalism, religious change, and intercontinental empires.

Previous chapters have looked at this topic through the themes of social and political organization, intercontinental relations, religion, and economics. This chapter focuses more on intellectual perspectives. Specifically, it explores the written records left by Africans who encountered Europeans and traveled outside the continent during this period. These encounters helped to shape their worldviews. To paraphrase the scholar Stuart Hall, in understanding the ways people understand their worlds and act within them, their international "routes" matter as much as their local "roots." The writers considered in this chapter had especially long intercontinental routes before they began to write, and many of them came to exist between worlds and to mediate among them in ways that are particularly cosmopolitan.

Today, with our understanding of the horrors of colonialism, we sometimes adopt a certain disdain for those early nineteenth-century Africans who took a middleman position between Europe and Africa and indeed often exhorted Africans to become more like Europeans. They are accused of having been "mentally enslaved" and "brainwashed" individuals who rejected their own identities and preferred to "mimic" those of Europeans. The women among them, like the female habitants of Saint-Louis and Gorée, are sometimes seen as having been mere concubines, sexual slaves, or greedy entrepreneurs. We wonder why they embraced aspects of European thought and life and did not see through the thin veil of "civilization" to the oppression it betokened for their children and grandchildren. Yet we have the benefit of hindsight. As late as 1870, formal colonialism did not yet exist for the vast majority of Africans. Moreover, close examination of their writing often reveals that these individuals *did* have misgivings about the operation of European power in Africa, if not always the ideas behind it. These African intellectuals were in fact often also patriots of their own people and were the precursors to the pan-Africanists and African nationalists who resisted and eventually brought about the downfall of the colonial system.

This is not to say that readers should necessarily leave this chapter celebrating al-Jabarti, al-Tahtawi, Boilat, Horton, Tzatzoe, and other European-educated or mission-educated African intellectuals of this era as heroes. Rather, I hope that readers might take away a deeper appreciation of their position in the world, the perspectives at which they arrived, and their attempts to promote projects they thought would help themselves and those around them.

EGYPTIAN INTELLECTUALS ON FRANCE AND ISLAM

One important set of cosmopolitan African writers in the early nineteenth century were Egyptian intellectuals, a number of whom traveled to Europe or encountered Europeans within Egypt. Their writings were often colored by the ambivalence created by Napoleon's invasion of Egypt in 1798 and Egyptian participation in the Anglo-French conflict on their own soil. On the one hand, many Egyptian thinkers came out of this conflict with a recognition of the need to modernize in order to resist future invasions, an impetus that culminated in Muhammad Ali's reforms of the 1820s and 1830s. They also understood that to do this they would need in part to emulate or at least learn from European science, technology, and perhaps humanities. On the other hand, the invasion in some cases prompted a deep distrust of Europeans and empowered conservatives who felt that their role was to safeguard Islamic and Egyptian values.

The French invasion itself was chronicled by the leading Egyptian historian of the day, Abd al-Rahman al-Jabarti. Al-Jabarti had been born in 1753 to a family of scholars who served as both teachers and interpreters of the law. As a young man, Al-Jabarti had chosen to record contemporary events as well as historical documents and to interpret them for other scholars. He continued this task in the diary he kept of events during the French invasion, the *Tarikh muddat al-Faransis bi Misr,* although he also edited and changed his interpretation in later versions of the diary. Within the diary, Al-Jabarti tried to explain French law and custom by interpreting edicts put out by Napoleon's forces. In one important section, he tried to explain French religion, and especially the particular revolutionary anticlericalism of Napoleon's forces. For the use of his countrymen, he chose to do so by reference to both the Islam and the Christian faiths present in Egypt. Thus he wrote that the French

are consistent with the Muslims in stating the formula "In the name of God," and in denying that He has a son or an associate. They disagree with the Muslims in not mentioning the two Articles of Faith, in rejecting the mission of Muhammad, and the legal words and deeds which are necessarily recognized by religion. They agree with the Christians in most of their words and deeds, but disagree with them by not mentioning the Trinity, and denying the mission and furthermore in rejecting their beliefs, killing the priests, and destroying the churches. (Moreh 2005, p. 28)

Al-Jabarti then moved on to explain French politics, and particularly the ethos and structure of revolutionary France, writing that "they have no chief or sultan with whom they all agree, like others, whose function is to speak on their behalf. For when they rebelled against their sultan six years ago and killed him, the people agreed unanimously that there was not to be a single ruler but that their states, territories, laws, and administration of their affairs, should be in the hands of the intelligent and wise among them." (p. 28) He also wrote that "they follow this rule: great and small, high and low, male and female are all equal." (p. 28) Yet Al-Jabarti noted that this rule was not actually always obeyed in operation, stating that "sometimes they break this rule according to their whims and inclinations or reasoning."

Finally, the historian moved on to something of an ethnographic survey of French culture, implicitly contrasting it to cultural norms in Egyptian society. He noted that "their women do not veil themselves and have no modesty; they do not care whether they uncover their private parts," and "whenever a Frenchman has to perform an act of nature he does so wherever he happens to be, even in full view of people, and he goes away as he is, without washing his private parts after defecation." He also claimed that "they have intercourse with any woman who pleases them and vice versa."

Al-Jabarti's interpretation of French cultural norms, political ideals, and religion represents an attempt to understand the invaders in the moment of invasion. Yet he did not at the time draw any implications for his own society. In the decades following the expulsion of the French and the rise of Muhammad Ali, however, his successors had greater time to do just that. One of the most significant of these was Rifa'a al-Tahtawi. As a young iman, al-Tahtawi was sent to France in 1826 as a member and spiritual guide of a group of more than forty Egyptians charged with learning French military and scientific technology, partly with the aim of starting a school of sciences in Cairo. The majority of these students came from wealthy elite families, many of them Turkic-speakers. While in France, they studied French literature and language before being divided into groups specializing in military science, engineering, chemistry, and in a few cases the humanities.

Al-Tahtawi studied astronomy, geometry, geography, physics, and math, although he particularly excelled in translation and both read and translated major French philosophical and geographic works. In 1831 he returned to Egypt, and in 1837 he was chosen to head the Cairo School of Translation. It was in this position that

al-Tahtawi came to grapple with the question of where to place Western "science" in the existing schools of Egyptian and Islamic scholarly traditions and theology. In struggling with this issue, he came to
express the ambivalence inherent in the merger. Al-Tahtawi's overall
solution was to understand Western science as a refinement of earlier
forms of Mediterranean scientific study—Ptolemaic Egyptian, Greek,
Phoenician, Abbasid, and Fatimid. However, he then argued that the
mechanics of science could largely be removed from philosophical
and historical considerations and be used largely as a tool of material and technological development. Yet he sometimes also spoke in
contradiction of this idea, depicting scientific enquiry as a product of
freedom and progress, and thus an instrument of social regeneration.
Through these contradictory formulations, he proposed that Egypt
adopt scientific knowledge and literacy from Europe but sought ways
to ensure that it should not replace local social structures. He rejected
both French scientists whom he saw as too secular and conservative
shaykhs and intellectuals in Egypt who turned their back on innovation as "extremists." In particular, he criticized the secular French scientists of the day for believing that "the intellects of their philosophers
and scientists are greater than that of the prophets."

Yet even while pushing for a moderate path of reform, al-Tahtawi
recognized that one could not simply meld two different worldviews
into one. Rather, he avoided the intense difficulties of integration and
advocated the adoption of chemistry, physics, and engineering education alongside religious study but not intersecting with it. In this
process, he saw his own role and that of his fellow intellectuals as both
promoters of science education and at the same time preservers of
Islamic law as a bulwark of social justice. Through their guidance, he
argued, Muhammad Ali could create a great nation in the context of
an Islamic enlightenment guided by religious scholars but promoting
science to create social renewal and build power.

THE ABBÉ BOILAT

Like al-Tahtawi, David Boilat was an African who traveled to France
as a young man and returned to grapple with the implications of his
experiences for his own society. Unlike the Muslim al-Tahtawi, Boilat
went to France to become a Catholic priest, and his encounter was
largely with other Catholics. Also, he returned to find not a growing
state but the beginnings of French colonial rule. Nevertheless, there

are some similarities as well as many differences between his voyages and findings and those of al-Tahtawi.

As a young Wolof-speaking man in Gorée, Boilat received his training from the globe-trotting French nun Anne-Marie Javouhey in a school she set up in Senegal in the 1820s. On her recommendation, he traveled to France following his graduation and returned as an ordained priest, or abbé. Upon his return in 1843, Boilat was assigned by the French governor Louis Bouet-Willaumez to start a secondary school in Saint-Louis. At the time, the French governor controlled only the island towns of Saint-Louis and Gorée and some small territories on the mainland. Bouet-Willaumez's hope was to create a class of assimilated Senegalese in these communities who would understand French law and culture. Boilat was generally a good ally in this pursuit, teaching his pupils Latin, European history, geography, mathematics, and European graphic design. However, the school thrived for only a few years, in part because of attacks on Boilat and his fellow African Catholic teachers by rival European missionaries. Following the failure of the school, Boilat moved on to new projects, most significantly writing *Esquisses Sénégalaisses*, in which he detailed the geography, economy, history, and "customs" of Senegalese peoples.

Unlike al-Tahtawi, Boilat seems to have believed in the advantages of fully adopting European culture and forms of Christianity. Thus he advised his pupils and their parents that students should speak only French, never Wolof, and should totally embrace Christian doctrines. He wrote that "with education you will see the flowering of commerce, science, art, religion, and above all an improved morality. You will see the fall of those gross, if not dishonourable, ways known as the custom of the country. You will witness the disappearance of all those absurd superstitions born of that silly deplorable gullibility with which most of the population deludes itself." (July 1968, p. 160) Guided largely by this faith, Boilat attacked Islam, which he saw as both spiritually misleading and a challenge to the civilizing influence of France.

Yet while Boilat seemed to have strongly adopted French and Catholic morals and values, he also identified the ways in which French colonial and Catholic Senegalese society seemed to be betraying those values. First, he leveled a critique at the French government for mismanaging its Senegalese possessions, pointing out that they had sent a series of governors to the colony—fourteen in seventeen years—all with different policies. He also complained of the administration's concentration on a strategy of large single-crop plantations, arguing instead for a peasant-run cultivation scheme. Finally, he criticized the upper classes of Saint-Louis, especially the French officials and their local wives, the *signare* class, whom he saw as being amoral and only passingly religious. Thus beneath Biolat's seeming assimilation lay the beginnings of a critique of French policy and colonial life.

JAMES AFRICANUS HORTON

While Boilat largely found himself interacting with French and Catholic ideas and values, there was a large class of literate West African intellectuals who intersected with British churches and institutions in Africa, Britain, and the Caribbean in the early nineteenth century. Many of these individuals began their formal studies in Sierra Leone, where schools had been set up by English-speaking missionaries from both Europe and the Americas in the early decades of the century. James Africanus Horton was perhaps the most outstanding student of these schools in his generation. The son of an Igbo-speaking captive

Jan Tzatzoe preparing to give evidence before the British Parliament, 1836. With him are South African Andries Stoffels, Reverend John Philip, and two other missionaries.

freed by a British naval ship and deposited in Sierra Leone, Horton studied at the greatest educational institution in the colony, Fourah Bay College, before moving on to the University of Edinburgh. Having completed his studies in medicine, he then joined the British army and returned to serve in the West African settlements, many of which were just forts along the coast.

Throughout his career, Horton appears to have largely accepted the idea that Britain was at the vanguard of civilization and that it had made great advances in technology, intellectual ideals, and religion that Africans would do well to emulate. In general, he felt that many coastal West African societies were entirely capable of attaining equality with Britain through such emulation. Thus he wrote, for example, that

> if Europe ... has been raised to her present pitch of civilization by progressive advancement, Africa too, with a guarantee of the civilization of the north, will rise into equal importance. The nucleus has been planted; it is just beginning to show signs of life and future vigour; it shoots out legitimate as well as extraneous buds. ... We may well say that the present state of Western Africa is, in fact, the history of the world repeating itself." (Horton 1970, p. 9)

Yet Horton personally experienced great racism and discrimination from Europeans both in Britain and in Africa. He especially fell out with several colonial officials on the Gold Coast who sought to sideline him and deny him advancement. Complaining of one officer under whom he had to serve, he lamented in a letter to the Reverend Henry Venn of February 3, 1860, that "to be prevented from doing one's rightful duty—to be received with the utmost coldness—to salute & don't receive a reply—to be deprived of quarter comforts—to have one's boy threatened to be flogged every day without just cause—to be prevented from cooking in half the fireplace in the officer's kitchen ... these are in brief language the sufferings I had to undergo since my arrival here."

A victim of racial discrimination, Horton also recognized racism as a growing trend in the British midcentury scientific and medical community. As a scholar, he sought to refute the allegations of African physical and mental inferiority that some British "scientists" raised. This he did largely by utilizing the critical scientific methods he had learned at Fourah Bay College and the University of Edinburgh. In a series of presentations and papers, Horton argued that the British scientists and doctors who published these studies often had not gathered their own data or conducted statistically relevant studies with proper controls. He concluded, therefore, that racial science was a betrayal of scientific process. In a letter to the *African Times* of April 23, 1866, he pointed out that the so-called scientists were "of prejudiced mind," and that they "select the worst possible specimens, and make them typical of the whole African race," whereas "when they attempt to describe the European race, no man comes to their standard but the most perfect and model form."

Because he was posted to many different coastal towns in West Africa, Horton was able to interact with a wide community of African intellectuals and to advise them on political projects like the writing of constitutions for local states and ways to influence the British government. Throughout his life, he urged these interlocutors to adopt many aspects of British science and culture. Yet he remained highly critical of a number of ideas emanating from Britain and of many of the officers and officials sent out to run British policy in the region.

THE "EDUCATED MEN" OF THE FANTE CONFEDERATION

One of the loose groups of African intellectuals with whom Horton interacted was the English- and Akan-speaking community of "self-made" men who organized much of the commerce that ran through the ports of Anomabu, Cape Coast, Elmina, and Saltpond south of the Asante state. In the nineteenth century, this region was a borderland between the British Atlantic and the Asante interior of the Gold Coast, and the local leadership opportunistically chose sides in the tug-of-war between these two giants. By the late 1860s, however, lines had hardened. Most of the coastal Akan-speaking communities now saw themselves as having a distinct identity, which they called Fante, and saw Asante as a great threat to their independence. These communities gradually chose to ally themselves with the British, perhaps not perceiving the possibility of colonialism from a faraway power. Only the coastal state of Elmina continued its close association with Asante, largely handling goods moving between Asante and the Dutch merchants of the atlantic who were an alternative to British traders along the coast and who set up offices in Elmina.

Along with local *ahenfo* (chiefly officeholders), the leading anti-Asante activists in this region were the self-described "educated men" of the coast. Many of these were Anglo-Fante, men (and a few women) of mixed heritage such as J. M. Abadoo, Robert Ghartey,

Joseph Dawson, George Amissa, George Blankson, and James Hutton Brew. These individuals were mostly merchants trading in palm oil, gold, and other goods from the interior and exchanging them for European cloth and metal goods. Some were also professionals like Brew, who was a lawyer. Others ran hotels and owned rural farms. They were generally acknowledged as local civic and religious leaders. Some served as deacons in the Methodist and other Christian churches, several were on the governor's advisory board for Cape Coast, and a number were related to local *ahenfo* and even in line to become chiefly officeholders themselves. Moreover, they were connected not only to each other but also to other African literati such as Horton and the influential Ferdinand Fitzgerald, the Sierra Leonean editor of the *African Times* newspaper. In general, they were Christians who believed in the economic "development" and "industrialization" of their own region. They spoke and wrote English very well and argued that the Fante were a "civilized" people, in contrast to the Asante, who often were portrayed as a backward and barbaric society. This last opinion, however, may have been more a promotion of their political views than a real estimation.

The "educated men" came to the fore of local politics in 1867, when a deal between Britain and the Netherlands threatened to give Asante more influence in the area. The actual revolt against the deal came first from rank-and-file citizens of the Fante states, who grabbed their guns and laid siege to the town of Elmina. The Fante *ahenfo* subsequently met in Mankessim, the town where Fante alliances and declarations of war were usually decided. The self-made men attended this meeting as well and managed to insert themselves into the discussion. They convinced the *ahenfo* that promoting the conflict as one between a modern, civilized society on the one hand and the barbaric Asante on the other would attract British support. Thus they caused a constitution to be written that unified the Fante into a single state with power shared between the chiefly officeholders and themselves. Modeled partly upon the British political and legal structure and partly on German efforts, this constitution went through a number of drafts, although it was never actually adopted. One draft proposed the following:

1. That there shall be a Legislative Assembly, and an Executive Council.
2. That the members of the Legislative Assembly be nominated by the votes of the people.

3. That the Legislative Assembly shall be composed of members representing the interests of the different states or districts of the Confederacy.

4. That it shall be lawful for the Legislative Assembly to make and establish all such Laws, institutions, and Ordinances as may be necessary from time to time for the peace, good order, prosperity, and good government of the Confederacy.

5. The said Legislative Assembly shall be dissolved at the expiration of two years from the date of its first sitting.

6. The said Legislative Assembly should be Composed of two Houses. One House being occupied by members representing the interest of the people and the other by the Chiefs—appointed by the King of the Confederacy. (3–8)

In the event, the project of creating a constitutional state based on European models failed for at least two reasons. First, this form of government did not attract the support of the mass of Fante-speakers, most of whom were willing to support a pan-Fante alliance to oppose the Dutch and Asante but were not interested in the European-style political structure proposed by the self-made men. Second, the British administrators were not won over by the constitution, but rather came to see the new proposal as a major threat. In fact, when a final draft was developed in 1871, the administrator immediately jailed the leaders, reportedly stating, "What do you mean by this? Do you not know that this is treason?"

Brew, Ghartey, and the other self-made men were among the first West Africans to experience a renewed British culture of expansion and empire that was just emerging in the early 1870s. Slowly, perhaps almost imperceptibly, European attitudes were shifting toward the formal imperialism and colonialism that would typify the next few decades. It is perhaps not unimportant that the Gold Coast would become one of the first extensive British colonies in West Africa in 1874. The limits of cosmopolitan Africa were being reached, and the realities of the segregation and discrimination that exemplified European colonialism were just becoming apparent in the region.

JAN TZATZOE IN BRITAIN

Southern Africans, however, had encountered the realities of a significant European presence long before the 1870s. Their experiences with settlers and officials were often very negative, but it was with Christian missionaries that they often had their most significant and ambivalent interactions. As we saw in chapter 3, the worldviews of many southern African people quite readily accommodated new political and religious realities. After all, identity in this region was quite flexible. For example, Xhosa communities often readily incorporated Khoisan-speaking groups, sometimes through conquest as well as assimilation. Moreover, there was a sense of religious syncretism here in which gods and ancestors from multiple groups could become quite easily mixed up. That made it quite possible, for example, for Christian practice and piety to become adopted into Xhosa society. Religious pioneers like the prophet Ntsikama brought these ideas to the fore partly by developing isiXhosa hymns around the theme of integration, such as: "The trumpet sounded, it has called us. As for his chase, He hunteth for souls. He, Who amalgamates flocks rejecting each other. He, the Leader, Who has led us." (Knox 1914, p. 62)As we saw in chapter 3, this integration could include such ideas as the apocalypse and the afterlife.

One Christian convert who interacted with missionaries, settlers, and officials alike was Jan Tzatzoe, a chiefly officeholder born in 1790. His father, Kote Tzatzoe, was a minor Xhosa chief. His mother was born a Khoisan-speaker, although her family was in the process of integrating into the local isiXhosa-speaking community. The younger Tzatzoe assisted several British missionaries in his youth, including a few who reported back to Britain on schemes by settlers and administrators to defraud Africans of their land in the Cape Colony. In 1836, he traveled with several members of the London Missionary Society to Britain to testify before a parliamentary committee investigating colonial treatment of subject peoples in the Cape Colony and elsewhere.

Tzatzoe's speeches and comments in Britain were recorded by local reporters and dignitaries. His observations included both his admiration for Parliament as a deliberative body and his impression of London as a peaceful town without drunkards or beggars. The British probably largely missed the relevance of these in the context of Tzatzoe's experiences in his own homeland. As a Xhosa leader of some importance, he would have been familiar with deliberative bodies, since both chieftainship and mission station protocol included councils of elders. He also would have been familiar with the very rough and rowdy frontier towns built by British and Afrikaner settlers and their local laborers, and could compare these to London.

His British audiences could not, however, have missed his critical comments made in speeches in London churches and meeting halls. While generally extolling the values that Britain brought to South Africa, especially Christianity, Tzatzoe also made clear his unhappiness at the subordinate place of Africans in the British Cape Colony and his aspirations for the future. In one speech, for example, he reminded listeners that "when we signed the treaty with the British Government at the Buffalo River, a paper was read which told us that we then became the children of the King of England, and that we were now British subjects. If we are the children of England, and if one with yourselves, let us enjoy the privileges of Britons." (423). He also complained of the abuses practiced upon Africans by officials and settlers, stating that "many Englishmen in the colonies are bad, but I will hardly believe that those Englishmen belong to you." (423). Tzatzoe may have had high hopes that his testimony and speeches would provoke some change, but they did not. Eventually, frustrated, he would return to lead his community in joining the Xhosa fighting the British in the War of the Axe, for which act he was removed from the church.

TOWARD COLONIALISM?

Tzatzoe and the other intellectuals cited here were all struggling with the changing global realities that would eventually drive formal colonialism. All of these writers, for example, recognized that European technology and science were reaching a point where for the first time they were seriously in advance of Africans' abilities to resist them militarily or economically. In seeking to redress this imbalance, these Africans were engaged in exploring the advantages of adopting aspects of European culture and technology. At the same time, however, they also to various degrees witnessed the contradictions within European claims to moral and "civilizational" superiority, although many of them ascribed this to "bad apples" rather than an immoral system. Their successors would be more openly critical, partly because many of them witnessed the trends of the late nineteenth century—the hardening of racial attitudes, the industrialization of killing, and finally the formal and violent conquest of the continent that heralded formal colonialism. These Africans—among them Bishop Samuel Ajayi Crowther, Edwin W. Blyden, George W. Johnson, William Wellington Gqoba, John Tengo Jabavu, John Knox Bokwe, S. E. K. Mqhayi, Tiyo Soga, and Kobina Sekyi—would plumb the questions of African identity and the challenges of surviving European rule in new ways and with new depth. Through their work the intellectual explorations of al-Tahtawi and Boilat would be expanded and become part of a body of African intellectual work.

At the same time, men like Tzatzoe and Horton also witnessed the closing of an age of freedom and cosmopolitan identities in Africa. Colonialism would bring with it a collapse of the flexible, assimilative system that allowed for great diversity and exploration in the eighteenth and nineteenth centuries. To serve the needs of colonial rulers, fluid ethnic identities would be hardened into "tribes." To help them collect taxes, frontier zones would become hard colonial "borders." In order to establish the colonial hierarchy, reciprocal relationships would be resolved into solid categories of race. All of this would mark a new chapter in the African experience, one that forms the basis of volume 4 of this series.

REFERENCES

Men and Women in the Middle?
Ayandele, E. A. *The Educated Elite in Nigerian Society* (Ibadan: University Lectures, 1974).

Zachernuk, Philip Serge. *Colonial Subjects: An African Intelligentsia and Atlantic Ideas* (Charlottesville: University Press of Virginia, 2000).

Egyptian Intellectuals on France and Islam
Livingston, John W. "Western Science and Educational Reform in the Thoughts of Shaykh Rifaa al-Tahtawi." *International Journal of Middle East Studies* 28 (1996): 543–564.

Moreh, Shmuel, trans. *Napoleon in Egypt: Al-Jabarti's Chronicle of the French Occupation, 1798* (Princeton, NJ: Markus Wiener, 2005).

The Abbé Boilat
Curtis, Sarah Ann. *Civilizing Habits: Women Missionaries and the Revival of French Empire* (Oxford: Oxford University Press, 2010).

July, Robert William. *The Origins of Modern African Thought: Its Development in West Africa during the Nineteenth and Twentieth Centuries* (London: Faber and Faber, 1968).

James Africanus Horton
Davidson, Nicol. *Black Nationalism in Africa 1867: Extracts from the Political, Educational, Scientific and Medical Writings of Africanus Horton* (New York: Africana Publishing, 1969).

Horton, James Africanus. *West African Countries and People* (Edinburgh: Edinburgh University Press, 1969; originally published 1869).

Horton, James Africanus, *Letters on the Political Condition of the Gold Coast* (London: Frank Cass, 1970; originally printed 1870).

The "Educated Men" of the Fante Confederation
Constitution of the New Fantee Confederacy", November 1871, reproduced in Parliamentary Papers XLIX of 1873, House of Commons printed series 11/3637, 3-8; and letter of 10 December 1871 in same, 3.

Kimble, David. *A Political History of Ghana* (Oxford: Clarendon Press, 1963).

Laumann, Dennis. "Compradores-in-Arms: The Fante Confederation." *Uhamfu* 21 (1993): 120–136.

Jan Tzatzoe in Britain
Bokwe, John Knox. *Ntsikana: The Story of an African Convert* (Lovedale: Lovedale Mission Press, 1914).

Levine, Roger S. "Savage-Born but New-Created: Jan Tzatzoe, Xhosa Chief and Missionary in Britain, 1836–1838." *Kronos: Journal of Cape History* 33 (2007): 112–138.

Special General Meeting of the London Missionary Society, *The Evangelical Magazine and Missionary Chronicle*, (London: Frederick Westley and A.H. Davis, 1863), 423.

Index